LITERACY

—— IS ——

LIBERATION

ASCD MEMBER BOOK

Many ASCD members received this book
as a member benefit upon its initial release.

Learn more at www.ascd.org/memberbooks

LITERACY
— IS —
LIBERATION

Working Toward Justice
Through
Culturally Relevant Teaching

KIMBERLY N. PARKER

Alexandria, Virginia USA

1703 N. Beauregard St. • Alexandria, VA 22311-1714 USA
Phone: 800-933-2723 or 703-578-9600 • Fax: 703-575-5400
Website: www.ascd.org • Email: member@ascd.org
Author guidelines: www.ascd.org/write

Ranjit Sidhu, *CEO & Executive Director;* Penny Reinart, *Chief Impact Officer;* Genny Ostertag, *Managing Director, Book Acquisitions & Editing;* Allison Scott, *Senior Acquisitions Editor;* Julie Houtz, *Director, Book Editing;* Megan Doyle, *Editor;* Thomas Lytle, *Creative Director;* Donald Ely, *Art Director;* Masie Chong, *Graphic Designer;* Circle USA, *Typesetter;* Kelly Marshall, *Production Manager;* Shajuan Martin, *E-Publishing Specialist;* Christopher Logan, *Senior Production Specialist*

PAPERBACK ISBN: 978-1-4166-3090-6 ASCD product #122024
PDF E-BOOK ISBN: 978-1-4166-3091-3; see Books in Print for other formats.

Quantity discounts are available: email programteam@ascd.org or call 800-933-2723, ext. 5773, or 703-575-5773. For desk copies, go to www.ascd.org/deskcopy.

ASCD Member Book No. FY22-5 (Feb. 2022 P). ASCD Member Books mail to Premium (P), Select (S), and Institutional Plus (I+) members on this schedule: Jan, PSI+; Feb, P; Apr, PSI+; May, P; Jul, PSI+; Aug, P; Sep, PSI+; Nov, PSI+; Dec, P. For current details on membership, see www.ascd.org/membership.

Library of Congress Cataloging-in-Publication Data

Names: Parker, Kimberly N., author.
Title: Literacy is liberation : working toward justice through culturally relevant teaching / Kimberly N. Parker.
Description: Alexandria, Virginia : ASCD, 2022. | Includes bibliographical references and index.
Identifiers: LCCN 2021048143 (print) | LCCN 2021048144 (ebook) | ISBN 9781416630906 (paperback) | ISBN 9781416630913 (pdf)
Subjects: LCSH: Culturally relevant pedagogy—United States. | Reading (Secondary)—Social aspects—United States.
Classification: LCC LC1099.515.C85 P37 2022 (print) | LCC LC1099.515.C85 (ebook) | DDC 370.1170973—dc23/eng/20211109
LC record available at https://lccn.loc.gov/2021048143
LC ebook record available at https://lccn.loc.gov/2021048144

30 29 28 27 26 25 24 23 22 21   1 2 3 4 5 6 7 8 9 10 11 12

To Elliott, Chloe, Caleb, and Clinton.

Put your crowns on, my loves.

LITERACY
— IS —
LIBERATION

Starting with Ourselves: Why Culturally Relevant Literature Instruction Begins with Us First

Our behaviors drive our beliefs.
—Elena Aguilar

Race is that big thing that some of us are comfortable talking about, and many of us aren't.

We should just begin there.

As a Black woman, I've always known I'm Black. When I move around in the world, my race is often the first thing people notice. Other indicators usually follow soon after, including my gender identity, and perhaps my ability, socioeconomic class, and others of the "Big 8" identity markers. (In case you're already feeling uncertain about these terms, know that I'll define them as we go.)

In the classroom, I'm often the first Black teacher my students— Black, white, and People of Color (POC)—have had in their careers (and likely might *ever* have given what we know about the whiteness of the teaching force). Yet, because they were often so inexperienced talking about race, these young people would talk *around* the topic: describing what I wore, or maybe something about my short hair or some other physical attribute. Rarely, if ever, though, did they say I was Black, even if they shared the same racial background. They lacked the confidence and practice of talking about race in a normalizing way, having become so acculturated to *not* acknowledging race that the practice was unfamiliar to them.

Inevitably when we started reading a text that featured a protagonist of color (again, often the first time they'd encountered accurate representations of themselves in a text) like *The Autobiography of Malcolm X* (Haley & X, 1965), they were willing to volunteer observations that dug beneath the physical surface. Finally, I heard them talking about a character's race, rereading descriptions about skin color that were written positively, seeing the possibilities and realities of themselves in what they read.

I like to tell people that I wasn't born "woke" or whatever language we're using to describe those we consider racially literate. In fact, I encounter moments that remind me that I have areas of willful ignorance, biases, or internalized racism all the time—daily, in fact. This process to get to a place where I understand systems of oppression, how I've been impacted (the good, the bad, and the ugly), and how that understanding directly affects my practice and the young people and preservice teachers with whom I work is not easy. At times, it can be exhausting and frustrating, especially when I'm called in by a dear friend for using language that is not inclusive (yup, it happens, and I'm also glad I have that friend who respects me enough to tell me).

Thus, we should make that admission: **if you want to be an educator who is grounded in culturally relevant instruction and who considers themselves to be a culturally relevant educator, you have to be willing to mess up and to continually strive to—and then *do*—better.**

What I know is that many educators want to do just that: they want to know how to take a hard look at what we've taken for granted and what has resulted in an educational landscape that is unequal for far too many vulnerable children. They want to own their part in it. They want to do better. Especially now. Especially *today*.

I know they do because they tell me, through emails, direct messages, and feedback at conferences and presentations. They ask for books: where to find them and how to teach them. They ask me to role-play what to do when a student challenges them about a racist moment in a "beloved" text (beloved by the educator, not the student). They ask me what they need to do, specifically, to become a co-conspirator for truth and justice, to make schools and other learning environments places where all children can thrive. Here, too, when I say *all* children, I really do mean *all* of them. No qualifiers.

I know that you, too, want to do this work of moving yourself and your practice into culturally relevant and racially just literature instruction. I imagine you're an educator, somewhere in your teaching career, at a place that has you questioning what you're seeing every day, when kids turn up disinterested in a book you *love*. You know there's something else out there for them; have even, perhaps, heard of "mirrors, windows, and sliding glass doors" (Bishop, 1990); and have a vague appreciation for what that means. Others might have had more than a passing interest in a department- or school-sponsored professional development about "diversity, equity, and inclusion" or "antiracism" that left you dissatisfied because you are all in but don't know what, exactly, to do next to effect immediate changes with the children and youth in your care. You know that becoming an antiracist, culturally competent literacy educator is more than a booklist.

This book is for you.

Together, I'm hoping we can have some "real talk," as the young people in my classrooms would often call for when they were ready to tell me the truth. Sometimes, that real talk was hard to hear: it held feedback about an instructional move that didn't resonate with them; it challenged me to learn from them; it made me go home, think hard, cry a bit sometimes, and return the next day renewed to, well, do better. It made me humble.

I'm working from a foundation that accepts you exactly as you are when you begin reading this book. Right now, you are an accumulation of your experiences—all of them, whether they be good or bad or somewhere in the middle. It's also my responsibility to make sure that you don't stay where you are. Lots of folks might get bogged down in guilt, shame, and blame as they begin to reconcile their privileges (which, again, we all have, and some have more privileges than others) with a liberatory life they want to lead. They might feel and believe, in the deepest parts of their souls, that all children deserve to read books that mirror their experiences in the texts, or that having an "ally" sticker posted visibly on their classroom doors signals solidarity, or that even by retweeting a BIPOC (Black and Indigenous Person of Color) person's words are important.

And yet.

We often can't get past those gestures into the more substantial work that must be done. We get squeamish when it comes to speaking up in department meetings about why it's time to reconsider teaching *To Kill a Mockingbird* and other problematic favorites. We look away or "don't hear" or "don't know what to do or say" when BIPOC children tell us about microaggressions they've experienced in our classrooms, often during the teaching of those texts. We might have completely sidetracked conversations about race because we found them too uncomfortable. We shut down attempts at progress, community building, or understanding, often because of our own fear, overwhelm, or personal discomfort. But some of us, too, are the first to say that we are "not racist."

Despite those reactions—(and I'm not here to judge you, but I am here to work with you to move into your power of being a thoughtful, vocal, racial equity co-conspirator)—you picked up this book, and you're still reading.

I have outlined a few descriptors of where you might be on your racial equity journey (and it is a journey, despite how trite that might sound; this work is never, ever done). Wherever you are at this current reading of this book is where you're supposed to be. For now. If you're still at that same point by the time you've worked your way through the book, though, then I've not achieved the goals I'd hoped.

To ensure we're clear about the overall aims for *Literacy Is Liberation* and what chapters address them, here's our roadmap:

1. You develop an understanding of the connections among behaviors, beliefs, and racial identity and are able to situate yourself within that understanding. (Chapter 1)

2. You can identify the characteristics of culturally relevant literacy instruction and know how to ground your practice within that framework and strengths-based literacy. (Chapter 2)

3. You know the qualities and values of a Culturally Relevant Intentional Literacy Community (CRILC) and are able to create one. (Chapters 3 and 4)

4. You are able to lead productive conversations about race, racism, and other topics with a range of students. (Chapter 5)

5. You incorporate specific high-leverage literacy practices that normalize the high achievement of all students, especially BIPOC students. (Chapter 6)

Now, after outlining the overall goals of the book, I want to circle back to why it's important for you to commit to doing the work of changing your literacy practice.

Starting with Myself

For many years, I insisted my students read the books I loved, or had been taught. Those books included *The Scarlet Letter, Macbeth, Frankenstein, Adventures of Huckleberry Finn,* and others featuring predominantly white protagonists. When my students—even the ones willing to suspend all annoyance with me because we had positive relationships—didn't engage with this "great literature" as I had anticipated, I was quick to blame them. I'm sure there were times I defended my positions to colleagues with something along the lines of "these kids need to know and have cultural capital" as I continued pushing them through the texts.

I was a Black teacher teaching predominantly Black and Latinx kids. I had more than enough savior complex to go around. I was sure that my belief in them and in the classics would be enough to catapult us all into (my own narrowly defined) stratospheres of success. It wasn't until I started listening to Black women mentors that I changed course and got serious about my own liberation. My dissertation advisor, Dr. Arlette Willis, pushed me to think about how my Blackness wasn't enough. More specifically, she challenged me to, for lack of a better phrase, "disaggregate my own data." Being Black meant more than sharing a similar melanin shade. I vaguely remember her posing a question in the margin of a draft I had submitted, as English teachers love to do, that said something like "What does this mean, exactly?" to what I thought was a complete sentence about being a Black teacher.

She pressed me to understand—and to articulate—that race and ethnicity are complex, multifaceted, and continually changing. Her push to change and expand my own understanding was essential to my critical unlearning about all the ways I've been impacted by white supremacy culture and how I'm still impacted daily.

Introduction to the Occasional Explanatory Comma
At some points in these first two chapters, I'm going to slow down and work through some important ideas. These "explanatory commas" are intended to build your background knowledge and are critical to culturally relevant literacy instruction. By no means are these explanatory commas exhaustive in their descriptions; rather, they're just enough to provide necessary context and encourage you to pursue further for your own personal growth. This additional work is required, ongoing, and work *you* have to do. It's not work you can, or should, ask a BIPOC or LGBTQIA+ or person who has disabilities to do for you.

White Supremacy Culture

Dismantling Racism (2021) defines *white supremacy culture* as

> the idea (ideology) that white people and the ideas, thoughts, beliefs, and actions of white people are superior to People of Color and their ideas, thoughts, beliefs, and actions.
>
> White supremacy culture is reproduced by all the institutions of our society. (para. 9)

What this means is that white supremacy culture is everywhere: in our schools, in our practices, in us. White supremacy culture is also inside systems and policies.

How white supremacy has worked on me. I know. I'm not white. However, I live my life in a city, a state, a nation, and a world that turns on the axis of white supremacy culture. Even Black, Latinx, and other People of Color can be impacted by white supremacy culture. After all, we all swim in the same water.

I was uncomfortable answering my professor's probing question about Blackness because, as much as I thought I was the same as my students, as I sat with my discomfort, I had to admit that

- My race is Black and my ethnicity is African American. Moreover, I was raised in the American South, by my grandparents on a farm.
- I was born into a working-class/working-poor family. Through education and profession, I'm middle class currently, while most of my family is not. It doesn't matter how uncomfortable admitting that makes me. That is my tension I constantly work through.
- I speak Standard White English (SWE). I don't speak any other languages, though I do understand Ebonics/Black English/ African American Vernacular English (AAVE). Note: I use AAVE and Ebonics interchangeably. Most of my family speaks SWE and Ebonics, with regional dialects, too.
- I am currently nondisabled, cisgender, nondenominational in my religious practices, queer, and a U.S. citizen.

Moving further inward, I needed to look closely at my own schooling experiences. I had Black teachers throughout K–12. I was a "good" student: I did my homework, took Advanced Placement (AP) classes, participated in student activities. Overall, I had positive experiences with my teachers. I was also one of a few Black students in my upper-level courses. At the same time, I read one or two books by Black authors in my high school career.

All of these parts of my experiences directly impacted, and continue to impact, how I see the world and how I interact with people, especially with my students. Yet, I cannot stop with this acknowledgment.

There's more work to do, still.

Let us remember the words of antiracist literacy expert Tricia Ebarvia (2019), who reminds us, "The internal work matters . . . a lot. You cannot disrupt if you don't understand how systems of oppression work. You cannot understand how systems of oppression work until you come to terms with how they have worked on you."

What that means is that there's something else that accompanies my story. I'll pinpoint a few instances to demonstrate how I internalized white supremacy. Being one of a few Black students in AP classes—while the majority of my high school peers who were Black were in general track classes—led me to think I was "special," that I was "different," that I was exceptional. I'm sure I thought I worked harder than my Black peers and that I deserved to be with my white peers because of that work ethic. I had internalized the false idea of exceptionalism.

As I look at those experiences now, I realize that I wasn't any more special than my Black peers. In fact, I'm sure many were much more hard working than I was. The dissonance was because they were "loud Black girls" or "aggressive Black boys" as we so often stereotype Black youth, and that was what teachers saw. Or, they practiced literacies that were unwelcomed in our classrooms, or they had white teachers who simply refused to acknowledge and encourage their brilliance. Systems that are designed to create difference are inherently unequal. As a result, I thought I was better when, in fact, I was simply living within, and benefitting from, a system as it operated.

More ways white supremacy has worked on me. Throughout my K–12 experience, and especially in high school, I thought my hard work was the reason I was in AP classes with so few, if any, other Black students. The majority of my Black peers were in the general track. Most likely, I'm sure I thought they were where they needed to be. After all, why would my teachers steer us wrong? Black and white teachers praised my work. My sense of self was attached to what my teachers and my peer group thought about me; for the most part, they thought I was a success. Consequently, I thought, that was true. More critically, I was most concerned with the feedback from white teachers and white peers. I valued their opinions about my intelligence, my performance, myself, far more than my family or my Black teachers.

I longed to have the looks and possessions of my white friends. I longed for their clothes that they seemed to acquire and discard so effortlessly. I wished my body would squeeze into a size 2 like my lithe, blonde classmates. While I can't say that I ever wanted to be white, I will say, now, that I wanted the ease and prosperity I thought my white friends enjoyed. And I thought that if I worked hard enough, that would give me enough cachet to be white adjacent.

Meanwhile, at home, I was loved by Black grandparents who had interrupted formal schooling because my grandmother had to take care of her siblings, and my grandfather had similar responsibilities to his family. My grandmother left school after 7th grade, and my grandfather had to leave after a few years in elementary school. Together, they raised eight children in jobs as a domestic (my grandmother) and a farm manager (my grandfather). My grandparents worked hard every day of their lives, making sure their children, and later their grandchildren, had what they needed, with occasional delights as they could manage.

Yet, at the time, I thought what they did was insufficient for me. I saw my life through what I didn't have, as compared to what my white friends had. Given that I wasn't white, I wanted to do all I could to gain proximity to whiteness. That meant being one of four Black students throughout my high school who were often the only Black youth in white spaces: parties, activities, courses. And while there were more interracial interactions in out-of-school spaces (athletics events, generally), my high school years were largely anchored in friendships with white peers where I was the "magical Black friend," as I've been called.

I enjoyed that role, as it allowed me to feel special, accepted. It didn't protect me from being called racial slurs on the school bus home, though. It didn't make most of my white peers want to understand anything about my upbringing. It *definitely* didn't make any of the white boys I crushed on want to take me to the prom (though one did, but he had to lie to his parents who otherwise would never have let him go to the prom with me, a Black girl). At the time, I simply did not have the language to express what was happening to me and how my coveting of white adjacency was my own internalized oppression.

As a result of that internalized whiteness and of my belief of the myth of meritocracy, I bought into thinking that if I worked hard, I could be successful. I could transcend my Blackness, essentially, by being exceptional. If I'd been able to view racism as structural, however, as it was and is, and if I'd had teachers who could have guided my burgeoning sociopolitical consciousness, I could have asked different questions:

- Why were so many of my equally—and even more brilliant—Black friends languishing in lower-track classes in the first place?

- Why did I have to find out about highly selective colleges outside the state by reading through a book about colleges rather than being encouraged to explore them by my high school guidance counselor, despite my solid academic record and range of extracurricular activities?

- Why weren't there more Black teachers in my high school, and why weren't there more Black teachers teaching those AP classes?

- Why did the school's elite STEAM program require a passing score on an entrance exam prior to entering the 9th grade, particularly given the uneven education of incoming middle school students from across the city?

- What had my white prom date's family been socialized to believe about their own whiteness and my Blackness that would make them unwilling to let their white son take me to the dance?

If I attempted to answer these questions on an individual racism level, I could attribute the answers to a few factors: a busy guidance counselor and discomfort. That's how individual racism works: it is perceived as individual acts between people, to be able to call someone a "racist" and spend lots of time on that level. Even at an individual level, these acts are still racist, as are the policies that allowed them to function.

However, structural racism was and continues to be at play through policies and systems. Quickly, I can mention a few factors: the entrance exam relied on a passing score that meant prospective students would have had a solid foundation in science and math courses from kindergarten through 8th grade. That is not the case for Black students in my hometown school district, as Black students' achievement has lagged persistently behind white peers. I was rewarded for obedience. I'm certain if I'd been one of "those loud Black girls," my fate would have been different. Again, we have years of data about the treatment of Black girls in school to indicate the relationship between disciplinary referrals and their academic progress (Morris, 2015). It's fair to think that my brilliant Black peers, especially the ones who were girls, were simply too loud and too, well, *Black*, for teachers to see beyond that. Teachers were unable to envision and value my peers' multilayered, complex selves as something other than one-dimensional and problematic.

Continuing to unpack these systems and how they worked on me—and, in some cases, how they worked *for* me—is lifelong work. My own internalized oppression caused me to devalue my Black grandparents' knowledge and brilliance because it wasn't "school" or "traditional," when, in fact, their tremendous funds of knowledge (Moll et al., 1992) enabled me and the rest of my family to have a foundation that has carried us, successfully, through generations of being Black in the United States in general and the American South in particular.

Also, on a structural level, the fact that they were alive, despite living in a southern state with a history of enslavement, with a family legacy of enslavement, and all the lasting impacts, was remarkable. Their lives were certainly made harder because of their limited formal educational opportunities because of racism and their Blackness. All the forms of structural racism they endured were linked. The marvel is that they, like many Black folks to this day, succeeded in myriad ways and that I am here to be able to tell the story.

I internalized what (mostly) white people thought about me. I didn't have the language to name and confront systems; rather, I thought that working even harder would lead to acceptance, which it never did.

I'm not white. I have, however, been impacted by white supremacy culture, individually and systemically. I work to undo the damage caused by white supremacy daily. I work at my liberation. I have to. As an educator and as a mother, it is imperative that I am firmly grounded in my liberatory and anti-oppressive beliefs, that I am able to confront my willful ignorance and lack of understanding when they show up (again, an ongoing process), and that I am able to use my beliefs to ground my practice so that I know I am teaching for transformation and liberation.

It is my hope that as you read this book, you'll gain some ideas about how to do this work for yourself and for your educational contexts.

Five Foundational Beliefs

Literacy Is Liberation is grounded in five foundational beliefs. These beliefs are important to understand and to return to throughout your reading as a touchstone for considering any sources of your own tension or hesitancy as you work on your own racial equity competence. Here, I identify those beliefs as a starting place.

1. **Humanity is not up for debate.** You'll often find that when an act of violence happens—when an unarmed Black person is killed by a white police officer, for example—there is hyper-focused

attention on the life of the victim. Their lives are scrutinized, speculated about, condemned. Essentially, the narrative quickly changes and the blame shifts to the person who was killed. In this book, we do not get into debates about a victim's past. Instead, I focus on everyone's right to live. When an unarmed Black, Latinx, or POC person is killed unjustly, all that matters is that. They had a right to be alive, and someone took that right from them. The blame and responsibility for that crime must remain squarely on the structures and systems that enabled that person who committed that crime.

2. **Racism exists. Anti-Blackness and anti-Black racism also exist.** There's enough research that has documented all the ways racism has functioned to maintain inequality. Thus, we operate from that understanding. Racism is at work in our classrooms, in our literature selections, in our conversations. It is everywhere. The Black Liberation Collective defines anti-Blackness as "the depreciation of black humanity, denial of black pain, and the obstruction of black agency, in a perpetual process of dehumanization. Anti-Black racism isn't merely ideology or overt prejudice and discrimination, but consists of mechanisms and practices that reproduce white advantage and Black disadvantages" (para. 03). Anti-Blackness can be perpetuated by other People of Color, by white people, and by Black people themselves.

3. **Black, Latinx, and POC communities have *always* valued literacy.** African American communities have pursued literacy even under threat of death. Literacy is something Black folks have considered integral to community progress: it is not simply an individual pursuit. Rather, through "freedom for literacy and literacy for freedom" (Perry, Steele, & Hilliard, 2003), one is able to teach and liberate others. Thus, saying Black and Latinx and other POC communities don't "value literacy" is simply untrue.

4. **White supremacy and white supremacy culture permeate everything we do, think, feel, and believe.** Every single person is impacted by white supremacy; it's unavoidable given the existence of power, racism, and oppression. For this reason, we will most likely spend our lives working on ourselves as we simultaneously work to eradicate it within ourselves as we dismantle systems that perpetuate inequality as well.

5. **We have to work actively, and in public, every single day if we want to be culturally relevant, antiracist people and educators.** Roxane Gay (2020) eloquently presses people to "[do] the difficult, self-reflective work of examining their own prejudices" (para. 18). If we're serious about becoming antiracist, our commitment is lifelong. Notably, progress isn't linear—we'll encounter areas of willful ignorance and make mistakes frequently as we push to end our own oppression and that of others. Also, this work has to be in public; it's not enough to extend support or appreciation for BIPOCs, especially when a BIPOC has spoken up and been ridiculed or dismissed. In a Learning for Justice (formerly Teaching Tolerance) workshop in 2019, Educator Valerie Brown urges us to "say the words before they get stuck in your throat." We can take that advice to remember to do the right thing out loud, despite our own perceived discomfort. That is what is required to be a culturally relevant educator. That is what is required to be a decent human being.

But What About Literacy?

You might be wondering why I've not spent much time talking about text selection, or teaching challenging texts, or creating diverse book lists. Believe me: the rest of the book focuses on these and other topics. However, none of these areas of focus matter without simultaneous work of unpacking your own beliefs about race, identity, and racism. Also, a "diverse" text in the hands of an assimilationist or segregationist teacher, to use the categories from Jason Reynolds and Dr. Ibram Kendi's (2020) *Stamped: Racism, Antiracism, and You,* has the potential to perpetuate a tremendous amount of harm for young people. Dedicating time to build your own racial literacy before turning to your curriculum can make your overall practice most effective.

Explanatory Comma: Racial Literacy

Dr. Yolanda Sealey-Ruiz (2021) defines *racial literacy* as

the ability to read, discuss, and write about situations that involve race or racism . . . Teachers who are able to engage their students in the topic of race are most successful when they employ self-exploration and honest assessments about the role they may play in perpetuating racist ideas. Once specific behaviors are recognized, it becomes easier for racially literate individuals to interrupt those behaviors in the future. Racially literate teachers develop curricula that are centered on fostering open-mindedness, commitment to inquiry and reflection, and exploration of ideas connected to the concepts of democracy and equity in schooling. (p. 2)

As we move through this book, you're going to be asked, and pushed, to develop your racial literacy. That is why I spent time earlier discussing some of the ways white supremacy has impacted my life—because those understandings, which continue to develop, determine how I see the young people and all the others with whom I work. As a Black woman, my ability to articulate how oppression has worked in my life helps me to become more comfortable and confident in naming the systems at work in my life and also makes me more able to interrupt and change them. It allows me to tell a more robust and accurate story of how I arrived at the point in my life where I am today. These understandings also help me to remember that, as Dr. Sealey-Ruiz says, I am *not* a victim.

My Early Literacy Experiences and Impact on My Teaching

It's hard for me to remember the books I read throughout K–12. I vaguely remember Edith Wharton's *Ethan Frome* in AP Literature and my infatuation with Jack Kerouac. I read *The Strange Career of Jim Crow* for my AP History class for a book club. I have no memories of reading any literature by anyone Black. However, at home, we had all sorts of Black books, ranging from literature to history. I think my grandmother's copy of John Hope Franklin and Evelyn Higginbotham's (1974) *From Slavery To Freedom: A History of African Americans* remains on the bookshelf of our house. We received the Black magazines *Jet* and *Ebony* regularly, which my grandmother would arrange in a thoughtful display on side tables and which I was responsible for dusting as part of my chores.

I was raised in a family of readers, with unlimited choice about what I could and wanted to read at home. My grandfather and uncles read what was of interest and necessary for them to do their work on the farm and in the trades, as well as what captured them: hunting, golf, fishing. My grandmother drove me into the city weekly for trips to the library, where I would stay while she ran errands in town. Thus, while my in-school experiences were limited when it came to independent reading and books that reflected my own experiences, I had a robust reading life outside school, enabling me to internalize messages that Black people valued literacy.

When I started teaching, I was firmly grounded in two beliefs: that young people needed to read what they wanted and that they also needed to read "classics." In my mind, both of those beliefs could exist, and for a while, they actually did.

I knew I wanted my first group of freshmen to read, and I knew I needed lots of books. The ones I gathered were often from donation centers, featuring white characters doing white things. It's a testament to the young people that they read them; I attribute that success much more to the relationships I had with them and my unrelenting demand that they read all the time more than their actual interest in the books. True, I had some books by Black and Latinx authors to mirror my students, but not nearly enough. (I now strive for numbers closer to 100 percent of BIPOC and #ownvoices texts.)

I was also guided by my own experiences of what I thought was "great and important literature." I wanted to make sure my students were fluent in classical literature so they could feel worthy and educated. Here, again, my own internalized oppression was notable. Core texts we read included *Macbeth, To Kill a Mockingbird,* and *The Odyssey.* I did to them the same thing my ELA teachers had done to me: I centered whiteness in the texts I chose and the decisions I made in teaching those texts. I'm sure my discussions about race were not well-structured because I was in the process of coming into my own racial consciousness. I taught my students as I'd been taught and as my graduate program modeled for me, and we never discussed race in any substantial, structured way.

I was afloat until Black women intervened and saved me. Through mentorship by Dr. Theresa Perry while I was still in the classroom and by Drs. Violet J. Harris and Arlette Willis while completing my doctoral work, I was able to think deeply about the beliefs I'd drawn on when selecting texts for young people and their impact. With equal parts love and intentionality, they connected me to the robust, enduring literary traditions of Black people in this country and why literacy has always been community driven, something

I realized my grandparents had also communicated. Dr. Perry named all the ways I'd been socialized into literacy by my grandparents and how I carried those historical lessons inside me.

They encouraged me to seek out and share texts that were written and illustrated by Black authors and illustrators, while also guiding my understanding and development of IPOC authors and illustrators, LGBTQIA+, and authors and illustrators with disabilities ("inclusive diversity," Dr. Harris urged). They were not ashamed that I had actively rejected my own Blackness and Black literature for so long; rather, they were thoughtful, loving witnesses as I came to consciousness and wanted to make up for lost time by reading as much as I could.

What remained consistent in those interactions was how each of those scholars intentionally and systematically handed over to me their love of Black people, traditions, scholarship, and texts. Under their mentorship, I have grown into the literacy educator my grandmother and some of my teachers probably hoped I'd be. Again, though, that process has not been linear, and I've had to interrogate how my own internalized oppression needed to be addressed, unpacked, and healed to be able to make better decisions for my students. I never would have been able to be here today, with you, if I'd not begun actively doing the work every day for myself. My own racial literacy enabled my ability to be a culturally relevant literacy educator.

Now More Than Ever: Why Being a Liberatory Educator Matters *Today*

I'm writing this book during what seems like a tipping point of a moment. As I write this, last week, George Floyd was murdered by a white police officer in Minneapolis. In protests around the world, people demanded justice for him, for Breonna Taylor who was killed by police officers in Louisville, Kentucky, for Toni McDade, a Black trans man killed in Florida, and what feels like a brutal roll call of so many others.

When I zoom in to see who is present at these protests, I have been shocked, for lack of a better word, to see so many white people standing with Black folks, demanding police reform and insisting Black lives matter. At the same time, Black and Latinx people have suffered disproportionately from COVID-19. Educators I know and work with are asking how to teach through this moment, despite feeling tired, unmoored, and confused.

They will not turn away.

Thus, long after the protests end, the question I have is, "What next?" What happens once they've exhausted all the books from the reading lists, followed all the Black, Latinx, and other People of Color on social media, even donated to Black creatives and causes? When they've returned to their classrooms and students who have also been experiencing this moment? On the other side of that, well, what remains?

Our students remain. Our colleagues remain. Our institutions remain. We cannot see these moments as separate incidents. True, the flames are now ignited, but how we choose to stoke—or extinguish—them is on us.

It's on us.

Educators tell me they would appreciate understanding how to select diverse texts, how to teach those texts, and how to address race and racism through texts in their classrooms. They sincerely want to teach *through* this moment, yet they are uncertain, afraid, immobilized. I get it.

Explanatory Comma: Culturally Relevant Pedagogy

The final explanatory comma for this chapter answers why this book is grounded in the theoretical principles and practices of culturally relevant pedagogy (CRP). Dr. Gloria Ladson-Billings (1995) developed CRP and has spent her career working with teachers and children to document the successful work of teachers of African American students. She explains her focus on African American children and youth—and my focus throughout this book primarily on Black children and youth—as "success among the 'least of these' tells us more about what pedagogical choices can support success" (p. 76). Modeling the best of scholars-as-learners, Ladson-Billings continues to revisit and update culturally relevant theory to keep it relevant to current contexts.

Ladson-Billings (2014) urges us beyond the surface of CRP, where, again, we can get stuck. She reminds us that true CRP must push students to "consider critical perspectives on policies and practices that may have direct impact on their lives and communities" (p. 78). Ladson-Billings also reminds us that "any notion of culturally relevant pedagogy has to change and evolve in order to meet the needs of each generation of students" (pp. 80–81).

As educators, we first require a deep understanding of how we have been shaped by policies and perspectives and how those same policies and perspectives impact the lives of our students and our practices. Thus, teaching is, and has always been, a political act. Especially in these times, we must acknowledge and teach through these moments and others as we provide the most excellent literacy instruction within our power to create and deliver to a range of students, and *especially* Black, Latinx, Indigenous, and POC ones who have traditionally been left out of full-scale considerations about raising the achievement for all students.

Ladson-Billings (2014) laments, "The idea that adding some books about people of color, having a classroom Kwanzaa celebration, or posting 'diverse' images makes one 'culturally relevant' seem to be what the pedagogy has been reduced to" (p. 82). She calls us to do the intentional work of becoming culturally relevant educators whose antiracist beliefs and practices improve our students' literacy outcomes.

What This Means for You and Our Work Together

I've spent some time explaining how I arrived here because modeling is important. When I'm with young people and adults, I aim to be my best, truest self. That self is also learning to breathe through discomfort and to tune in to my emotions. I think I've also benefited from mothering a Black sun (spelling intentional) who has big feelings of his own. Someone once told me that unless I actively work to do something different, I would end up parenting him the way I was parented. And while I always knew I was loved, I was also raised in a family that wasn't big on outward displays of affection or on feeling all the feelings. Instead, we stuffed them down, never processed them, and were astounded when those emotions showed up in other says. For me, that was through eating and struggling with body image and acceptance throughout my life.

The phrase "get comfortable being uncomfortable" comes up all over the place, almost as a mantra. It's neither easy nor comfortable being uncomfortable, in my experience. I understand how these words can land as a platitude, rather than as an insistence on sticking with something personally difficult when distraction or shifting the blame is *so much easier* (this might be the moment, too, where we spend an inordinate amount of time looking at memes, or "procrastibaking," or doing something else that allows us to do anything other than sitting with discomfort). As avoidance strategies, those work brilliantly, but you're not really going to ever become a liberatory literacy educator, if you allow yourself to do that. What I will assure you is that, if you view your discomfort with curiosity and compassion, seeking to understand what is beneath those feelings, then you will experience breakthroughs.

Each chapter includes at least one Takeaway and To-Do's, prompts intended to help you process the key understandings and a call for you to commit to some type of purposeful action. The more you practice and actively work to live through the ideas in this book, the greater the potential of internalizing different, anti-oppressive ways of living, teaching, and learning. Also, backsliding is possible and to be expected. I, too, have felt that I have finally "gotten it" or made some sort of progress on recognizing or understanding something about my own practices. I might even have wanted some sort of award or prize. Seriously—I have. I have even wanted to share my "new" understandings in ways that were insensitive and, well, *not* best liberatory practices. For example, my knowledge of the diversity within Asian American history, culture, and contemporary experience is growing. I have so much to learn and am learning and unlearning regularly. Every one of my new "discoveries" is not to be shared with my Asian friends. If anything, I need to sit with why it's taken me so long to learn this information in the first place and what I need to do to make sure I know more and can teach that to my child and my students. I need to take this information and put it into a broader spectrum of how learning about others' experiences help me to understand my own willful ignorance—note, I originally used the term *blind spots* but changed it because it's ableist language—and how much more I need to learn. There is *always* more to learn.

I share stories throughout this book where it makes sense, largely because I can be skeptical about taking anyone seriously if they don't demonstrate some type of vulnerability and honesty, especially when it comes to racial justice work. Also, through stories, we can *explore our narrative power*, to quote the Center for Story-Based Strategy, and can also consider the myriad ways our stories can help to push against systems.

I also aim to be forthcoming to say that this narration and story sharing can be a tremendous amount of emotional labor for BIPOC folks to do under the white gaze. Please remember that my stories are just that: mine. I am not obligated to lay myself bare to allow you to witness the scars of my oppression. Instead, I share stories directly related to the work the book is asking you to do—asking *us* to do— to help you understand what it can mean if you engage fully.

I can imagine that you have lots of stories of your own to tell, and will have many more to tell, in your own journey. Tell your stories. I also hope you'll begin to critically view those stories through a lens of how they have shaped you and how they have helped you see the world. Getting comfortable telling these stories also helps you to develop your understanding first of yourself and then of your practice—a critical literacy storytelling, if you will, aimed to think deeply about all the ways oppression has worked on you, for better or for worse. Then, we can be able to show up ready to pursue the equity and justice that our students deserve. In the next chapter, we look closely at culturally relevant pedagogy as our foundation for building our literacy practice.

Takeaway

It's our personal responsibility to commit to being liberatory, racially literate literacy educators. Through thoughtful, consistent actions that are grounded in an understanding of systems, we can work through understanding the impact of living within a racialized and racist society. Simultaneously, we can apply that understanding to our practice. This process begins with an acknowledgment of and a commitment to doing the

sustained, lifelong work of becoming antiracist, culturally relevant literacy educators.

To-Do's

Use the eight identities to describe yourself: race, ethnicity, sexual orientation, gender identity, ability, religion/
spirituality, nationality, and socioeconomic status. Digging
deeper, think about which identities take precedence during
particular situations or with particular people (your dominant
identities), and spend time considering the implications of
that decision. How have you been able to enact power through
those identities? For example, if you identify as white, in what
ways have the privileges associated with whiteness worked
in your favor? If you were to do a deep dive into a few of your
subordinate identities, what would those identities be and what
would you learn? As you sit with those identities, where do you
notice discomfort? How can you hold that discomfort with curiosity? How might understanding those subordinate identities
help you to fully understand your identity and which areas of
self-development you need to do?

Digging Deeper
into Culturally
Relevant Pedagogy

*You can't do one or two [parts] and say, "Oh, I'm being
culturally relevant." You've got to do all three things.*
—Gloria Ladson-Billings

In this chapter, we will spend a bit more time unpacking culturally relevant literacy instruction as the key theory for understanding the why of our literacy work. With that foundation, we can then turn to specifics that lead to a change in literacy design in the following chapters. What I have come to understand is that there are many incomplete understandings and misunderstandings of culturally relevant pedagogy, making for its similarly loose and incorrect implementation of theory and practice. This chapter, then, aims to make sure we all have a shared understanding of the foundation on which this book rests.

Thus, our learning objective for this chapter is to understand the big ideas of culturally relevant pedagogy—academic success, cultural competence, and the development and increase of sociopolitical and critical consciousness—to prepare ourselves for doing transformative literacy work in our classrooms.

Culturally Relevant Pedagogy: The Foundation

What I find compelling is that when I went back to reread the work that has influenced and helped me locate my own teaching beliefs, Ladson-Billings's work still resonated and affirmed me. It also remains current and critical to our work today. More recently, Ladson-Billings has updated her theory to include culturally responsive and sustaining pedagogies to reflect a changing world. Yet, many educators who desire to be culturally relevant/responsive/sustaining/antiracist (all theories that build off Ladson-Billings) struggle to articulate what these theories mean for our everyday work, making meaningful action steps challenging. I suspect that much of the difficulty of understanding and being culturally relevant means we must practice all of its elements all the time.

It is helpful to think of culturally relevant pedagogy as the larger framework that grounds many of the beliefs about equitable instruction. It is our throughline. More specifically, Aronson and Laughter (2016) help us to understand the association between culturally *relevant* pedagogy (Ladson-Billings) and culturally *responsive* pedagogy (Gay) as a relationship between teaching (the doing) and pedagogy (the approach or central understanding and belief). I draw on both scholars in certain cases during this discussion. Aronson and Laughter explain:

Gay's focus on teaching primarily seeks to influence competency and methods, describing what a teacher should be doing in the classroom to be culturally responsive. Ladson-Billings's focus on pedagogy primarily seeks to influence attitudes and dispositions, describing a posture a teacher might adopt that, when fully embodied, would determine planning, instruction, and assessment. Although many researchers use these terms interchangeably, we think it important to differentiate the two for focusing on two separate but complementary types of outcomes: *teaching affects competence and practice whereas pedagogy affects attitude and disposition.* (pp. 166–167; emphasis mine)

We can have a strong foundation for how literacy then figures into that work if we hold on to understanding the theory that drives our practice.

The Three Big Ideas of Culturally Relevant Pedagogy

Ladson-Billings (in Fay, 2019) helps situate us in the continuing importance of culturally relevant pedagogy—or, as Aronson and Laughter say, our "attitude and disposition"—and its three essential tenets that impact how we should approach our teaching. She also articulates what we should hold on to (and what has remained consistent since she created the theory) as we try to figure out how to situate culturally relevant pedagogy with other theories. Ladson-Billings argues:

I've never changed it. What's changed is the way people have interpreted it. But I defined it as a threefold approach to ensuring that all children are successful. That approach requires a focus on students' learning, an attempt to develop their cultural competence, and to increase their sociopolitical or critical consciousness. (para. 10).

In short, the three legs of CRP, according to Ladson-Billings, are *academic success, cultural competence,* and *sociopolitical/critical consciousness.* One has to do all three or else it's not culturally relevant teaching.

Notably, Ladson-Billings insisted on focusing on African American students who were successful and their "exemplary teachers." She expressed that her own desire to conduct her research was to challenge "deficit paradigms" about Black students. In fact, Ladson-Billings (1995) asserts that "a culturally relevant pedagogy is designed to problematize teaching and encourage teachers to ask about the nature of the student–teacher relationship, the curriculum, schooling, and society" (p. 483). We must *always* be thinking about and questioning our beliefs and relationships with our students. However, it can sometimes be difficult to problematize our teaching and ask those questions that improve our practice because asking equity-based questions will likely surface responses that can make us uncomfortable. We must ask them anyway.

This is where Dr. Geneva Gay's culturally responsive pedagogy helps.

Explanatory Comma: Culturally Responsive Pedagogy

Geneva Gay directs us to understand the specific work teachers can—and must—do, and *how* to do it. Essentially, she sharpens Ladson-Billings approach. Gay (2010) explains:

> A very different pedagogical paradigm is needed to improve the performance of underachieving students from various ethnic groups—*one that teaches to and through their personal and cultural strengths, their intellectual capabilities,*

and their prior accomplishments. Culturally responsive teaching is this kind of paradigm. It is at once a routine and a radical proposal. It is routine because it does for Native American, Latino, Asian American, African American, and low-income students what traditional instructional ideologies and actions do for middle-class European Americans. That is, they filter curriculum content and teaching strategies through their cultural frames of reference . . . [making them] more personally meaningful and easier to master. It is radical because it makes explicit the previously implicit role of culture in teaching and learning, and it insists that educational institutions accept the legitimacy and viability of ethnic group cultures in improving learning outcomes. . . . The close interactions among ethnic identity, cultural background, and cognition are becoming increasingly apparent. . . . It is these interactions . . . that give source and focus, power and direction to culturally responsive teaching. (pp. 26–27; emphasis mine)

Gay demands that we understand our students' cultures through their multiple and intersecting identities and that we see them through an assets-based lens. This understanding then helps us to create instruction that responds meaningfully to those identities, and that helps students understand they are the *center* of our curriculum.

Gay helps us think broadly about culture, explaining her own varying definitions as "I often shift between using the term itself [*culture*] and its equivalent meanings. Instead of simply saying 'culture,' I will sometimes say 'values, attitudes, and beliefs,' 'customs and traditions,' 'heritages and contributions,' or 'experiences and perspectives,' all of which I consider as equivalents of 'culture'" (2013, p. 52). What is consistent in Gay's definition and understanding of culture is that it encompasses a range of traits that can help us to dig more deeply into understanding our students. Gay's definitions of culture and culturally responsive teaching insist on seeing culture as a positive, as an asset all our students bring to class with them. Her broad definitions also push us to understand the myriad, complex facets of culture and how critical the link is between understanding culture as an integral part of being culturally relevant educators.

To help synthesize Gay's assertions, we can ask ourselves, What do we really know about our students' identities and cultures (knowing that there is no singular identity or culture for anyone)? What do we know about their values, attitudes, and beliefs? What do we know about their experiences and perspectives? How do we know that for sure that we are not relying on stereotypes or assumptions?

Also, no group of students is the same. For instance, simply because students might appear to be of African descent does not mean they all share a common identity. We must figure out the range of experiences our students have, and we can do that through conducting family interviews, spending time in local communities, and building our own understanding by reading books written by authors, illustrators, and other artists who share the backgrounds of our students, for example. It is *our* responsibility to learn without making our students teach us. Given that meaningful relationships drive our work with students, it's also critical that we learn about their families and communities. We need to be as interested in learning about them as we are about any other parts of our practice. Now, we move forward, carrying Gay's articulation of culture and culturally responsive pedagogy with us, as we return to the broader concepts of culturally relevant pedagogy.

Culturally Relevant Pedagogy and Action Steps for Our Practice

Again, Ladson-Billings reminds us that the key beliefs of culturally relevant pedagogy are academic success, cultural competence, and sociopolitical/critical consciousness. In the next section, I look more specifically at how educators can interpret those big ideas.

Academic Success

Students don't have to choose. "Culturally relevant pedagogy must provide a way for students to maintain their cultural integrity while succeeding academically," Ladson-Billings explains (1995, p. 476). Students should not have to negotiate between who they are and how they identify to be successful in our classrooms. That means we do not shame or punish them for expressing their identities. We do not limit their exposure to only texts that do not provide them with a range of representation. We do not punish them for showing emotion or for expressing developmentally appropriate behavior. Instead, we realize that brilliance can show up in all kinds of ways, and we make space. We take seriously our work of truly knowing and loving our students, understanding that such acceptance and love encourages them to be their academic best.

An educator is responsible for _all_ of their students' success, setting a challenging academic horizon for achievement and teaching for mastery. Ladson-Billings (1995) notes that the teachers she observed "each . . . felt that helping the students become academically successful was one of their primary responsibilities. . . . Students were not allowed to choose failure" (pp. 475, 479). Teachers had a stake in their students' success, taking it as their personal responsibility to make sure all students in their care were academic achievers.

Seeing ourselves as responsible for the mastery of *all* of our students is a powerful baseline.

In our work as educators, personal responsibility for our students' academic success means evaluating and reevaluating our curriculum, materials, and expectations to make sure that we see children's inherent brilliance. It's notable here also to remember that many Black, Latinx, and other students of color are systematically underrepresented in gifted and talented, honors, and Advanced Placement classes. Teacher recommendations and observations often play a part in these decisions. Another moment of reflection can be to think about what our personal role has been in making these recommendations or not making these recommendations. What do our patterns suggest about our beliefs? It's imperative that we explore our own practices and ask ourselves difficult questions that will surface our beliefs. We must make sure we are not serving as gatekeepers that deny students advanced academic opportunities simply because we cannot reconcile our own biases with the need to normalize high achievement for our BIPOC students.

Gay (2013) provides an additional level of thinking when she poses questions teachers need to ask themselves about their students and what they believe about their potential. We should regularly return to these questions, asking them at different points throughout the year, reflecting if our answers indicate our commitment to all of our students' success. She asks:

- What do I believe are the underlying causes of achievement difficulties of various culturally diverse students?
- Am I able and willing to articulate and scrutinize my beliefs about cultural diversity in general and about particular ethnic groups?
- Can I discern how specific beliefs about different ethnic populations are embedded in particular instructional decisions and behaviors?

- Am I willing to consider making significant changes in my attitudes, beliefs, and behaviors, and, if so, do I know how to proceed? (p. 144)

We have to grapple with these questions. Gay (2013) summarizes, "Positive attitudes about ethnic, racial, and gender differences generate positive instructional expectations and actions toward diverse students, which, in turn, have positive effects on students' learning efforts and outcomes. Conversely, negative teacher beliefs produce negative teaching and learning behaviors" (p. 56). It's critical, then, that our attitudes and beliefs align with our instructional aims in positive, liberatory ways.

Moreover, educators are responsible for selecting and teaching a challenging, relevant curriculum that centers the highest beliefs for what their students can attain. Consider Perry and colleagues' (2003) claim: "To tell students that they are smart and to repeatedly teach content that is not intellectually challenging affirms that in reality the students are not seen as smart or intellectually capable" (p. 103). Far too often, educators don't create literacy tasks that have a high level of academic press and that are intellectually challenging. Low-level reading comprehension questions, rote tasks, five-paragraph essays with teacher-generated thesis statements, and outdated textbooks with racist information come to mind as examples.

When students respond, however, by calling our instruction boring or by showing their dissatisfaction through disruptive behavior in some instances, they are often punished for those expressions, especially if they are BIPOCs. Instead, we should be grateful they are giving us feedback on what is not working for them, thank them for that feedback, and immediately change our instruction. We need to be attuned to our students' needs and committed to their success while they are in our care (and, for many of us, long after they've left our classrooms, too).

The Danger of Lowered Expectations

Teachers should regularly audit their curricula to determine if the tasks they are requiring of their students are rigorous, relevant, and aligned with their students' cultural identities and backgrounds. We simply do not aim high enough for our BIPOC students. We should assume that *all* of our students are gifted and talented and work diligently to make our materials, lessons, and assessments reflective of those understandings, providing necessary scaffolding and supports for all students to be successful. Again, we first must believe, in our core being, that BIPOC students *are* gifted and talented already.

Take a moment and think about your own undergraduate experience.

I often am guided by thinking, "What do I have to do to make sure students are able to succeed academically and, more broadly, at my undergraduate institution (Colby College in Waterville, ME) or a similar place?" Not a ridiculous question for me because it helps me to aim high and to design challenging instruction. I'm not demanding that my students attend that particular college or take a particular path after graduating from high school, but I do want them to have that option if they so choose. Rather, what I am suggesting is that often we are limited by our own expectations for students that are not ambitious enough. It also helps me to remember that many Black and other POC students are often "undermatched" when they are considering prospective colleges (Hoxby & Avery, 2012). Many could attend, and be successful, at highly competitive colleges and universities if they only had people who believed in them and helped them get there. Why can't that person be you?

Although all students should be able to determine their own postsecondary school plans, it is still worth considering what it would take in their time with us to develop necessary competencies that can prepare them to be successful in your own undergraduate institution.

For instance, I was a double major in English and American studies and needed to be able to read challenging material, to generate ideas based on evidence and opinion, to participate in discussions that required thinking on my feet, and to meet deadlines. I also needed to be secure in my own identity to be able to navigate a predominantly white, wealthy institution. Thus, if I back-mapped those skills to a sophomore year scope and sequence, I would be guided by making sure whatever I was asking students to do would provide language and rationale for the expectations, explicit instruction, and practice. My horizons extended beyond our year together, to think about young people long after they'd left my class. This thinking and horizon holding is an example of planning using high expectations. The day-to-day work is designing learning experiences that help them achieve mastery.

Many BIPOC students who attend systematically underfunded schools have been regularly confined to lower expectations and deficit thinking. But that doesn't have to be the case. If we are truly serious about being culturally relevant educators, we must want, push, and teach for more for our students. While we raise our own expectations and challenge our own beliefs about what they can do, we also get busy welcoming all of our students into our learning spaces, which takes cultural competence.

Cultural Competence

Ladson-Billings (2001) explains cultural competence as follows:

> Teachers who are prepared to help students become culturally competent are themselves culturally competent. They do not spend their time trying to be hip and cool and "down" with their students. They know enough about students' cultural and individual life circumstances to be able to communicate well with them. They understand the need to *study the students* because they believe there is something there worth learning. They know that students

who have the academic and cultural wherewithal to succeed in school without losing their identities are better prepared to be of service to others; in a democracy, this commitment to the public good is paramount. (p. 97).

Ladson-Billings demands teachers be culturally competent as part of our work of becoming culturally relevant educators. In her definition of cultural competence (2014), she says, "Cultural competence refers to the ability to help students appreciate and celebrate their cultures of origin while gaining knowledge of and fluency in at least one other culture" (p. 75). Based on this expectation, what work must teachers do?

She is first calling us to action to dig into what we have come to believe, value, and practice about our own cultures (it might be helpful to recall Gay's broad definitions of culture). She pushes us to think about how we have been socialized into communities we belong to and how race, power, ability—all the big 8 identifiers—have functioned within those spaces. We also need to be thinking about our students, what we know, and what we need to know about them and their communities as we develop our fluency about their experiences, too.

Cultural competence and whiteness. Given the whiteness of the teaching force, cultural competence means, specifically, that white teachers must understand their own white identity, the ways that whiteness has worked in their lives, and the ways that whiteness continues to work in their lives.

Certainly, we all have different experiences and whiteness, as any other race, ethnicity, gender, and so forth, is not monolithic. Thus, everyone will have different stories. However, many white educators have only begun to think about how they as white people are "complex social actors with dynamic histories" (Miller & Tanner, 2019, p. 11). The fields of critical whiteness studies and white teacher identity studies offer ways forward. We need to remember that, as Miller and Tanner remind us, "whiteness has variability," and that "our anti-racist work in classrooms, without an understanding of the deeply rooted nuances of racism, could likely backfire" (p. 20). In other words, until white educators come to a fully racialized understanding of their whiteness and how racism works as a result of whiteness and white supremacy—which requires ongoing, substantial internal work—cultural competence is unlikely to be successful.

The racial uprisings that began in the spring of 2020 resulted in an abundance of resources that help white people do that work, and I encourage white readers to avail themselves of those, and continue to avail themselves of those, as understanding and dismantling whiteness and white supremacy is most likely a lifelong pursuit. And, as we know, if we are indeed committed to culturally relevant instruction, and to being culturally competent, working to understand one's whiteness is the most urgent work to undertake. (The appendix includes helpful resources.)

Cultural competence and linguistic justice. Language, and languages, are happening all around us, all the time. Within cultural competence is a respect and understanding of the power of language, especially Black English/African American Vernacular English (AAVE)/Ebonics and other varieties of English that we all speak. For instance, as a native Kentuckian, my friends and family speak White Mainstream English (WME), AAVE, and regional dialects of both, depending on where we are located within the state and with whom we are speaking. In Boston, again, depending on which part of the city you are in, you'll hear a broad range of languages and dialects, all being spoken simultaneously.

However, AAVE is often deemed inferior. In its position statement on Ebonics, the Conference on College Composition and Communication (CCCC; 2020) of NCTE states, "Ebonics reflects the Black experience and conveys Black traditions and socially real truths. Black Languages are crucial to Black identity. Black Language sayings, such as 'What goes around comes around,' are crucial to Black ways of being in the world. Black Languages, like Black lives, matter" (para. 04). We all speak dialects of English. White Mainstream English is, indeed, a dialect, just as AAVE is, yet AAVE is frequently used as a marker of Black speakers' intellect. When students speak AAVE in our classrooms, they can be told their language is "incorrect" and "wrong," and educators can incorrectly assign assessments of lower intelligence to those students. Actually, we are incorrect or wrong, and our response indicates our failure to understand that AAVE is a systematic, rule-governed language deeply tied to identity, culture, and Blackness. Cultural competence means that we have a nuanced understanding of AAVE and its importance to Black identities.

To understand this aspect more fully, I draw on some of the principles from the CCCC's (2020) position statement, especially that teachers "stop teaching Black students to code-switch." Code-switching has long been suggested as the way for Black students to assimilate into our ELA classrooms (it's a belief I held and practiced, too, until I took a deep dive into the tenets of Black linguistic justice). In our demands for students to code-switch, we are still centering one language as deficient (AAVE) and another as superior (White Mainstream English). More specifically, as the CCCC position statement demands, we need to stop teaching students to code-switch because "this approach does not celebrate and love on Blackness and Black Language. In fact, when teachers force Black youth to code their language, it is a form of anti-Black linguistic racism" (para. 11). Our refusal to name racist systems and validate students' languages creates substantial harm.

The CCCC position statement challenges us to first name anti-Black racism and linguistic racism. Then, too, we must be prepared to take on the suggestions of the document to change how we understand, teach, and value Black English and Black Language. This work is urgent, though, if we want to be culturally relevant and responsive educators. Because Black Language is so deeply tied to Black identity, we must learn how to value, center, and celebrate it in our classrooms as well, if we are really to have ELA classrooms that value the achievement of all of our students. Unpacking the CCCC demands for ourselves, first, is a powerful starting point.

What is required is a study of AAVE, both for ourselves and with our young people, both of which I have done and continue to do. For example, teachers can first guide students to understand the beauty and rules of the language through a close reading of novels such as Zora Neale Hurston's *Their Eyes Were Watching God* or Angie Thomas' *Concrete Rose*, and then can lead conversations about distinguishing between AAVE and slang because they are *not* the same (which is always eye-opening for students because they've never had the time and space to discuss language in these ways). Then, because I want to support students' developing sociopolitical consciousness, they have specifically facilitated conversations about racism and AAVE, what it has meant to devalue Black English in schools, and suggestions for change.

I've had high school seniors teach a graduate class where they shared their knowledge with preservice teachers, helping those mostly white teachers develop their own understandings—and correct their misunderstandings—about AAVE. Centering these studies of Black Language, and letting students lead the way, has been a powerful way for them to demonstrate what they learned and why it mattered. Students also had a different perspective of Black Language after studying it—they knew how racism impacted language, and they were able to engage in discussions and action that aimed to rectify those injustices. They were on the path to feeling they didn't have to choose which dialect to speak in our classroom. However, many had spent years of their education being told speaking AAVE was incorrect—a reminder that culturally relevant teaching must be systematic to prevent damage to BIPOC students that cannot be undone in a single school year.

Black Language is not the only language vilified in schools. I use it as an example because of my own positionality as a Black woman, my work with Black students, and also the seemingly unending linguistic violence enacted on Black students as we demand they assimilate without addressing the bigger issues of ending anti-Black linguistic racism. However, any student who does not speak WME and enters classrooms where teachers do not have experience either understanding or teaching about linguistic racism faces the same challenges. If we use Black Language as a case study and draw on the demands from the CCCC position statement to move us to action, then we can change our practice for all students who speak, and should be allowed to continue to speak, a broad variety of languages. (Most likely, we as their teachers speak a variety of languages too, remember.) The work I've done with young people about AAVE that I described earlier is an example of what engaging young people around issues can look like, and it gets us into the third pillar of culturally relevant pedagogy.

Development of a Sociopolitical and Critical Consciousness

Critical and sociopolitical literacies are the most important literacies. Students are problem solvers. "We can't maintain democracy without engaged citizenry," Ladson-Billings (2021) reminds us.

Teachers are instrumental in helping and supporting students' approach to how they look at the world and situate themselves within it. Ladson-Billings (1995) notes, "Not only must teachers encourage academic success and cultural competence, they must help students to recognize, understand, and critique current social inequities" (p. 476). In CRT classrooms, teachers help students question, challenge, and process their worlds. A teacher is a partner as students "construct, deconstruct, and reconstruct" their learning (Murray & Milner, 2015, p. 900). Teachers have to deliberately help students develop the ability to notice, critique, and change the world around them. Indeed, this expectation *is* political. *Teaching* is political, and as educators charged with preparing children and young people to be active citizens in a global democracy, we must equip them with the tools to critique, change, and thrive in that world.

Critical literacy is directly tied to agency: we guide students so they can realize how much power they have. Eventually, too, we can get out of their way and let them lead (or continue leading) because we've intentionally supported the growth of their critical consciousness.

Murray and Milner (2015) further urge:

> Students in PreK–12 classrooms develop a critical consciousness that they move beyond spaces where they simply or solely consume knowledge without critically examining it to transform inequitable societal conditions. The idea is that teachers create learning environments where students develop voice and perspective and are allowed to participate (more fully) in the multiple discourses available in a learning context by not only consuming information but also through helping to deconstruct and to (re)construct it (Freire, 1998). (p. 900)

The development of critical consciousness insists that teachers believe students have a voice, and that our role as teachers is to nurture those voices. This is an acknowledgment that might be difficult for some to comprehend, especially if we've grown accustomed to thinking we know what's "best" for students. This resistance can be considered paternalistic or adultist, however, as both practices deny BIPOC students power and agency. If we strive to be culturally relevant educators, though, making sure students know how to question, critique, and create change is vital. They also need regular practice developing these habits and dispositions. In fact, creating different futures is paramount for our students. Agency, or active participation, is something educators often fail to acknowledge that BIPOC students exercise, but it is something all students have.

2020 was a year when we had the opportunity to see the power of youth organizing and how dynamic sociopolitical consciousness can be. Many of the protests about the killings of unarmed Black Americans by police officers were led by youth. In a webinar hosted by Teaching for Change, co-editor of *Teaching for Black Lives* Jesse Hagopian (2020) said, "The students of today are becoming the educators. They're teaching us what solidarity, courage, struggles, and victory can look like." Hagopian urged educators to "encourage [students] to share their stories with us," asserting that, as they are living through these moments, they need educators to "provide context, [help them] to make sense of anti-Blackness, and scaffold difficult conversations" that include police violence and institutional racism.

Providing context is important. These painful moments are prime for engaging young people in processing what they are seeing and also in connecting them to a broader timeline—in this case, of racial rebellions and responses. However, that is *not* a time to inflict more trauma on BIPOC students by forcing them to relive the horror of public lynchings make them suffer through "debates" about a victim's humanity. Instead, our work is to help our students make sense of their worlds in a constructive, thoughtful way that helps them to process their experiences and to know they have the power to change systems and participate in our democracy.

Despite our settings (virtual, in-person, hybrid, or some shifting combination of those), what remains consistent throughout these situations is that our students need our help to process the moment that we are living through, especially if we want them to be change-makers. Also, this is why we must be culturally competent and able to discuss structural racism, mass incarceration, policing, and other topics that are often present in the lives of BIPOC students. It's unacceptable to refuse to center our students' development of sociopolitical consciousness, especially in such fraught times, and to help them understand the power they have as youth to organize and create different futures, in the same ways youth have throughout history.

I used book clubs to help high school juniors anchor themselves within this moment of racial uprisings during the summer of 2020. They could choose to read texts that included *Just Mercy* (Stevenson, 2014) and *The Other Side of Freedom: The Case for Hope* (McKesson, 2018) for book club discussions with their peers. The questions they generated from their readings were wide-ranging and powerful: these were young people who were simultaneously attending marches, signing up to speak in online community meetings, and supporting family members who were struggling with COVID-19, which disproportionately impacts BIPOC communities.

Young people needed to process what they were experiencing and their place within this powerful movement. I was able to provide the context through historical examples that included the work of organizers Ella Baker and Fannie Lou Hamer, Ava Duvernay's documentary *13th* about mass incarceration, and other relevant sources. Students also regularly brought in their own resources, including organizing a virtual visit with a lawyer from Bryan Stevenson's Equal Justice Initiative (EJI). This historical grounding strengthened young people's understandings about the present and highlighted how often it was young people, working collectively in intergenerational communities, who have demanded political change, while the EJI visit helped clarify many of their whys. My job during that time was, as Hagopian defined, to provide the context, to scaffold the difficult conversations, and to give them the time to process their experiences. It was also my job to recognize, lift up, and celebrate the work of young people creating the worlds they want. They remind us, certainly, that hope does remain.

Takeaway

Ladson-Billings is clear about what is required to be a culturally relevant teacher. We must be relentless about ensuring all of our students are academically successful as we teach for mastery of challenging, engaging material—for every single student. We must be culturally competent, meaning we are fluent in our own culture and those of our students. This requirement of fluency means that white teachers must have a deep, nuanced understanding of their white identity. Finally, culturally relevant educators support their students' development of a sociopolitical and critical consciousness. We listen to our students and their questions, and we provide a frame of historical context and support for conversations that help them process their experiences, activism, and agency.

These three pillars are foundational to be culturally relevant educators, which is why I've spent time in this chapter highlighting them. All three must be ever present, or else it's not culturally relevant teaching. Now, as we turn to culturally relevant ELA instruction, we think next about working with our students as we construct literacy communities with them in support of their brilliance. Also, because the field of culturally relevant pedagogy is substantial, I close this chapter with some suggestions for additional reading about each of the points to encourage further reading and learning (see Figure 2.1).

To-Do's

Spend time thinking about the three foundational parts of culturally relevant teaching—academic achievement, cultural competence, and sociopolitical consciousness. In what specific ways is your practice already aligned with culturally relevant teaching—what examples can you provide? Which of these three areas is the most difficult for you to practice? What concrete steps can you take to make progress to become culturally relevant in this area, as well as the other two?

What are the issues directly affecting the communities in which your students live? Who are the local leaders and organizers creating change around those issues? What meaningful actions can you learn about and support within your students' communities? Think about the texts in these communities (newspapers, technology, other aspects of material culture) and what they help you to learn as well. How does reading these texts help you to gain a fuller understanding of the community and cultures that might accompany students into your classrooms?

Culturally relevant pedagogy is foundational to understanding culturally sustaining pedagogies (Alim & Paris, 2017) and the more recent abolitionist teaching pedagogy (Love, 2019) and antiracist teaching. As you read about other pedagogies that draw on CRP, determine which of their tenets are consistent with CRP and which are points of departure. Evaluate which parts of your existing practices fall into any of these pedagogies and where you would like to either add or strengthen to make your practice fully culturally relevant and responsive to your students and your teaching context.

FIGURE 2.1

More Resources for Culturally Relevant Teaching

Academic Achievement

Ladson-Billings, G. *The Dreamkeepers: Successful Teachers of African American Children.*

Ladson-Billings, G. *Crossing over to Canaan: The Journey of New Teachers in Diverse Classrooms.*

Siddle-Walker, V. *Their Highest Potential: An African-American School Community in the Segregated South.*

Cultural Competence

Dunbar-Ortiz, R., Reese, D., & Mendoza, J. *An Indigenous People's History of the United States for Young People.*

Hong, C. P. *Minor Feelings: An Asian American Reckoning.*

Michie, G. *Holler If You Hear Me: The Education of a Teacher and His Students.*

Ortiz, P. *An African American and Latinx History of the United States.*

Rogers, S. J. *They Were Her Property: White Women as Slave Owners in the American South.*

Sociopolitical Consciousness

Watson, D., Hagopian, J., & Au, W. *Teaching for Black Lives: Rethinking Schools.*

Lindstrom, C., & Goade, M. *We Are the Water Protectors.*

McGuire, D. *At the Dark End of the Street: Black Women, Rape, and Resistance—A New History of the Civil Rights Movement from Rosa Parks to the Rise of Black Power.*

3

Defining Culturally Relevant Intentional Literacy Communities (CRILCs)

*You cannot change any society unless you take
responsibility for it, unless you see yourself as
belonging to it, and responsible for changing it.*
—*Grace Lee Boggs*

What is a culturally relevant intentional literacy community?

In this chapter, I define the essential characteristics of a culturally relevant intentional literacy community (CRILC). It's important to first understand how I'm defining community more broadly before we zoom in on literacy and the classrooms we want to create with our students.

Our objectives for this chapter are

- To develop a shared understanding of the characteristics of a community in general;

- To identify what the qualities and values are of culturally relevant intentional literacy communities.

Defining Community

In its simplest form, a *community* is a group of people who come together around shared purposes. Communities are also interdependent, described by activist Adrienne Maree Brown as places where members "all need something from each other and they all provide something to each other" (2021, para. 139) If many of us have learned anything during the pandemic that upended every part of our lives, it was probably about how much we missed connection with others. We missed our communities. They are places that support the goals of connection, interdependence, and often survival for those within them.

We are not blank slates. We enter into communities bringing all of who we are, even if, in more structured spaces, "all of us" isn't necessarily welcomed. For many Black, Latinx, Indigenous, and other POC children, being denied community can be devastating. Without a supportive, culturally relevant community and an educator who is holding the center, we know what happens. The astronomical suspension and expulsion rates for Black girls, the number of Black boys pushed out of early childhood experiences, and the policing of Black and Brown bodies through strict dress code policies disrupt the formation of an authentic community that values the experiences of all children. When children are suffering or excluded in classrooms, there is no community, and conditions for their success are missing.

While we start with the understanding that a community is composed of people with shared interests, we have to deepen our understanding to include members' needs for connection, interdependence, and the belief that a community—and the work required to create and maintain it—are necessary and possible. Brown (2021) reminds us, "If we believe in community, then we must get curious about the ways we need to grow and communicate in order to truly be a part of the community. Not just one community, but the multitude of communities we intersect with" (para. 06). Creating a community must be intentional if we want it to be liberatory. Curiosity can help us understand that communities are built through practice, engagement, and participation. Within school-based environments, it is the educator who is responsible for assuring classrooms contain these general qualities and others specific to a particular discipline, such as literacy, as they invite students to join them.

Literacy in Community

Literacy best happens within a community because students are able to take in, respond, and learn in relationship to each other. Literacy has a social function.

Think about if you've ever been in a book club and how you interacted with other members. What do you remember about the books you read? Are those memories stronger than the experiences of being with your friends and the lasting feelings of sharing space and time together? This social connection and desire for a shared experience is a key component of gathering with others. Classroom literacy communities can function similarly. As we most likely took care to find our members, select what we read, maybe even thought deeply about how we wanted folks to feel while part of that book club, we need to also extend the same care to thinking about what we need to do, as educators, to intentionally cultivate feelings of belongingness, spaces for disagreement, and an overall sense of interdependence for the youth in our literacy classrooms.

Professional literacy organizations also help us to understand literacy as relational. In its position statement "The Act of Reading: Instructional Foundations and Policy Guidelines," the National Council of Teachers of English (2019a) states, "Reading is a sociocultural activity in which readers construct meaning from text through the lenses of culture and personal experience" (para. 01). Students are more likely to experience success if their basic needs for community are met first (i.e., they feel connected to those within the community, they feel valued, and they feel part of a shared purpose). In these literacy spaces, the same tenets of culturally relevant practice are always present, working simultaneously. It is up to committed teachers to intentionally envision their classrooms as a community of transformative literacy first, and their role within that community. No decisions are left to chance.

Now, we can look specifically at the qualities of culturally relevant intentional literacy communities to create a framework for decision making.

Culturally Relevant Intentional Literacy Communities: Overview

A *culturally relevant intentional literacy community* (CRILC) is a space where educators work deliberately with students to create a literacy environment that systematically normalizes the high achievement of everyone within that community.

In CRILCs, the three foundational pieces of community are present (i.e., connection, interdependence, and necessity), as are all three components of culturally relevant pedagogy (i.e., a focus on students' learning and achievement; development of their cultural competence; increasing students' sociopolitical and critical consciousness). CRILCs provide the additional layer of direct actions and values that improve the literacy lives and achievement of the students and teachers within them. The next section explains each value and action and includes action steps to help teachers begin creating CRILCs in their own classrooms.

Values of CRILCs

CRILCs have three predominant values that bring the principles of community and cultural relevance together. CRILCs

- Are asset-based.
- Encourage and nurture vulnerability.
- Are driven by collectivism and sociopolitical change.

CRILCs are asset-based. Learning about the talents and experiences our students already have when they walk into our doors is imperative to being culturally relevant. After all, it's difficult to create a community if we don't take the time to know who is in that community, or if we rely on our own assumptions about who we *think* is in our community.

We see the world through our own racialized, gendered, complicated lenses. We also must acknowledge that our lenses are biased and that we don't always have a complete understanding of something because of that bias (take Harvard's Implicit Bias surveys to learn more). We see our students through those same lenses (and they, in turn, see us through their own lenses). Accordingly, we can fail to acknowledge the powerful attributes our students bring with them to school and can, instead, see them as deficits unless we actively work to confront our biases.

Yet, we don't have to see our students this way. It's useful to draw on the theory of "funds of knowledge" (Moll et al., 1992) to reframe our thinking. In this study, researchers worked with Latinx households and communities to determine the "strategic knowledge and related activities essential in households' functioning, development, and well-being" (p. 139). Teachers—who were trained in using ethnographic methods by the researchers who conducted the study, meaning they were attuned to observing and listening—were not casual observers who visited their students' homes on fact-finding missions. They were not going to count the number of books inside a family's home, for instance. Instead, teachers were learners, collaborating with families and exchanging ideas.

One important finding from Moll and colleagues' study is that the people with whom children interacted possessed a multidimensional understanding of a child. They report:

> Thus, the "teacher" in these home based contexts of learning will know the child as a "whole" person, not merely as a "student," taking into account or having knowledge about the multiple spheres of activity within which the child is enmeshed. In comparison, the typical teacher–student relationships seem "thin" and "single-stranded," as the teacher "knows" the students only from their performance within rather limited classroom contexts. (pp. 133–134)

These teacher-learners were intent on learning *from* and *with* families, creating a two-way stream of communication that centered the experiences of their students' households. Students were not separate from their communities. This intention, and the actions of home visits and observations of students' family networks, established a level of trust with families that helped create a different relationship between home and school. These visits were also an opportunity to understand the rituals and traditions and everyday knowledge that are part of community life, as they also can be points of resonance in classrooms as we work with our students.

How might our own literacy practices benefit from adopting this same perspective? What might our spaces look like if we aimed to make them places that are thick and multistranded? CRILCs are these places. It is far too easy to see children as deficits, especially when we use measures that are strictly ones that do not center their funds of knowledge. For instance, we can see a group of Black youth as "struggling readers" because they fail to meet our expectations for engagement without considering all of the broad ways they practice literacy or how they understand those practices. We can think Latinx or other young people come from "families that don't care about them" because we haven't attempted to humble ourselves and learn from what all families have to teach us. We might not understand the linguistic fluency some of our other IPOC students have because we shrug and think they "simply refuse to speak English" without challenging our own biases and lack of understanding about linguistic fluency. These assumptions are deficit-driven and harmful to students, families, and any attempts we might have to be culturally relevant or to build community. Our beliefs have to change if we want to work from an assets-based framework.

When we humble ourselves and learn from and work with families and students, though, we have a powerful opportunity to engage with them as the experts of their experiences and bridge these home and school literacies in a productive, powerful way. In our literacy work, we can use our broad understandings of multiliteracies to catalogue the vast literacy practices our students have, using that knowledge to invite students into our classrooms as partners, as collaborators, and as valued members of our community.

This information is critical for knowing who our students are, how they experience the world, and how educators develop an intentional community with their students. Adopting an initial stance of humility and openness to learning from families, followed by a thoughtful noting of all of the ways that families and children participate in complex networks of care and support outside school, and finally seeking to understand those networks and participation within them as strengths, is foundational to culturally relevant practice.

Dr. Ernest Morrell provided a powerful way to ask students how they have processed the pandemic. In a tweet (2021), he suggested, "What if we asked every kid in America next fall as an assignment to tell us what they learned during the pandemic, how they grew, how they are different, and what they wanted to do next? They could represent this multimodally and share within the community!" The answers to these questions can help educators think about how students define their own learning experiences, in their own words, while providing us with feedback about how to help them process and center those experiences in our work. Also, when we have actual data from our students, we can work from a strengths-based orientation and use that insight to develop and respond to the community's needs.

When we recognize and value our students as imbued with funds of knowledge, we see them differently. We see them from a lens of ability and possibility; we know they enter our classrooms teeming with stories, with strengths, with their full humanity. Then, as educators, our work is to figure out how to center our students as we work together to achieve educational excellence, so that we can make our classrooms and our understanding of our students thick and multi-stranded, too.

Too many BIPOC students, however, are never allowed even to be acknowledged as human because of our own racism and biases. If we cannot mitigate that racism and bias then we cannot change. If we change how we think we know our students, however, into *actually* knowing them, we get closer to equity and liberation. Thus, actively interrogating, then reframing and changing our own beliefs about our students is the first value of CRILCs.

To-Do's

Asset mapping has been described as "the general process of identifying and providing information about a community's assets, or the status, condition, behavior, knowledge, or skills that a person, group, or entity possesses, which serves as a support, resource, or source of strength to one's self and others in the community" (Advancement Project, 2012, p. 6). Conduct a collaborative asset-mapping of your students' communities. Find a central location within your classroom to record and reflect about what everyone learns. This asset map should be a dynamic document, prompting discussions about strengths and ideas about potential equitable actions community members find important to them, as well as an invitation to substantial conversations about systemic challenges and opportunities.

CRILCs are places where vulnerability is necessary. Vulnerability is at the heart of CRILCs. Researcher Brené Brown (2020) explains vulnerability as, "The emotion that we experience during times of uncertainty, risk, and emotional exposure. It's having the courage to show up, fully engage, and be seen when you can't control the outcome" (p. 23). Learning, in its most profound form, requires vulnerability.

Community members—children and youth, educators, parents, and caregivers—all show up with their own experiences, histories, and aspirations. For many BIPOC young people, by high school, literacy often has become a chore, associated with reading texts that don't resonate with their experience or that haven't offered opportunities for exploring "windows, mirrors, or sliding glass doors" (Bishop, 1990). Windows are texts that provide us with an understanding of lives or experiences unfamiliar to us, mirrors are texts that reflect back to us our myriad experiences, and sliding glass doors are texts that can also be transformative for the way they change us as readers. Additionally, we know that our students practice a range of literacies in out-of-school contexts (NCTE, 2019a) that are not recognized or validated in classrooms. Thus, when we ask our students to enter our classroom spaces, we must remember that they could be carrying shame about the mismatch they have experienced between their literacies and our expectations for them. Through our beliefs, our actions, and our curriculum, however, we can lessen those feelings of discomfort if we are willing ourselves to be vulnerable first and then to support our students' vulnerabilities, too—but not exploit those vulnerabilities.

We also cannot expect students to be vulnerable because we want them to be. Indeed, while students are not their trauma, we must acknowledge the harm that education may have caused our students. Working through these experiences requires time and establishing genuine trust established on students' own terms, which is a particular type of vulnerability in itself. When students are vulnerable with us, we should accept that as a gift and work diligently to protect and preserve that trust.

As educators, we have to model being open to hearing *all* of our students' experiences. If we are responsible for causing harm—through our failures to listen to our students, through our curricular decisions that have inflicted curricular violence (Jones, 2020), or through our own biased practices—we must address and heal that harm. We must also continually audit and evolve our practices so that we are regularly reflecting and repairing these areas while being proactive to avoid causing future harm. We must believe in the work of CRILCs enough to assume responsibility for our words, our actions, and our texts and to actively create equity outcomes that honor and value the literacy lives of our students. None of that healing is possible without vulnerability, though.

Because we *will* make mistakes, we demonstrate vulnerability through addressing and repairing them. I make mistakes all the time: I don't tune in to students. My adultism gets in the way and causes me think I know better than they do about what they want to read and enjoy. I don't actively address issues of power consistently. I've confronted a long list of mistakes throughout my teaching career. I have caused harm. Fortunately, restorative justice provides some guidelines for how we can address that harm. The Deep Center (2020) frames restorative justice as follows:

> Restorative justice is a proactive community-building strategy that creates a culture of love, justice and support in which all members

of a community feel valued, connected and able to thrive. In this sense, restorative justice is fundamentally a culture rather than a mere set of protocols. It is a culture that uproots the causes of harm before harm happens. When harm does occur, restorative justice responds by gathering people to form a community of account-ability and deeper relationships. (p. 5)

Restorative justice is an interactive process that is deeply vested in accountability and the addressing and prevention of harm for its members. It is not only limited to handling conflicts, though, especially if we think of it as a culture as the Deep Center defines it. In CRILCs, principles of restorative justice can normalize vulnerability and create productive, equitable literacy communities because they support the addressing—and eventual prevention—of harmful beliefs, practices, and interactions that can get in the way of everyone's success.

Restorative justice—and its particular guiding questions—can elicit feelings of shame as we interrogate our biases, decisions, and the harmful impacts on our students. It is our work to accept the emotions that might arise to move through our shame and take actionable steps so that we rectify harm and learn from our mistakes to change our practice.

To-Do's

Spend some time exploring the principles of restorative justice, especially the guiding questions that include "Who has been harmed?"; "What are their needs?"; "Whose obligations are these?"; and "How do we collectively work to put things right?" (Lyons, n.d.). How might these questions guide your philosophy of being in community with students in a classroom? What are the specific beliefs and practices you hold/have held that have harmed your students? What actions do you need to take to rectify that harm? What agreements do you need to make to assure you will do your best to cause no further harm? What will accountability look like for you?

CRILCs are driven by collectivism and sociopolitical change. Abolitionist Mariame Kaba (2021) defines collectivism as a practice and a belief: "We can't do anything alone that's worth it. Everything that is worthwhile is done with other people" (p. 178). Within a collectivist space, as we envision and shape our CRILCs to be, everyone is guided by a spirit of belonging to one another, of being responsible to one another, of being invested in the long-term flourishing of one another. In CRILCs, the group is more important than the individual. This means that successes and challenges are viewed from a perspective that responds to the interconnected needs of the community. While a collectivist belief might be hard to embrace, especially given much of white supremacist patriarchal capitalism's focus on the individual and competition, it's important for us to understand the damage that happens when we let the individual's needs supersede the needs of the community.

Or, to quote a popular athletics saying: "There's no *I* in *team*."

An educator understands the individual's needs within the community and can hold and respond to them as well, recognizing that collectivism also helps ground the community in equity. Fortunately, this collectivist orientation means that the teacher is invested in the group's success.

BIPOC young people often shine in collectivist spaces. They can express their opinions in writing and in other formats that make sense to them (think about all the ways youth leverage technology regularly and how those forms of technology can support learning objectives here). Helping young people shift from blame to action is critical, and this move can be strengthened by first reading and thinking about organizations who are creating more equity, then asking students to connect and dream about doing action-oriented, solutions-driven work themselves. An educator's next steps must always be to lead students to challenge and refashion something different, collaboratively, and CRILCs can be the places where an equitable literacy experience is centered and practiced by all within it.

Everyone is also located in the sociopolitical moment, meaning we teach through the times, for better or for worse. We simply cannot ignore the everyday. I'm always reminded that young people live in the world as do I, every day bringing those experiences with them and often needing guidance about how to process them. Thus, even if we are personally hesitant to, say, talk about Black Lives Matter, or to verbalize why our classrooms need to be queer-affirming spaces, our students need us to talk and teach about those ideas.

Ladson-Billings (Fay, 2019) explains the importance of sociopolitical and critical consciousness as follows:

> A hallmark for me of a culturally relevant teacher is someone who understands that we're operating in a fundamentally inequitable system—they take that as a given. And that the teacher's role is not merely to help kids fit into an unfair system, but rather to give them the skills, the knowledge and the dispositions to change the inequity. The idea is not to get more people at the top of an unfair pyramid; the idea is to say the pyramid is the wrong structure. How can we really create a circle, if you will, that includes everybody? (para. 12)

Ladson-Billings is challenging us to explicitly name unfairness and injustice with our students, pushing us to also interrogate systems. A good place to start is inside our classrooms to recognize what systems of inequity are present and need uncovering. This is an initial step that prepares collaborative work with students that follows.

In CRILCs, challenging injustice might mean a teacher leads a series of discussions with students about tracking and about the racial demographics of students in "college prep," AP, and honors classes (as I have). They might analyze data from the school's National Report Card, even comparing that data to other schools to provide a robust understanding of their experiences. Then, a teacher can help students to understand systems that have continued to perpetuate educational inequities, while also encouraging students to vocalize their experiences within the systems and determine audiences and other outlets for their counternarratives that help challenge data, stereotypes, and other assumptions. Here, too, it's important to link students to organizations, official and unofficial, that are examples of spaces where BIPOC children and youth thrive, so they have tangible examples of what different spaces look like. As equity scholar Ijeoma Oluo suggests, we should help students to think through the questions, "How do we interact with these systems and what change can we make?" (Ayers, 2020), then work with them to change what is possible given their spheres of control and influence. And something is *always* possible.

A teacher can next turn to the texts assigned in these courses: What might students have experienced reading them? What do they think about representation and opportunities for them to see themselves reflected in their assigned reading? Was there any opportunity for them to read "mirrors and windows" (Bishop, 1990)? Again, it is important that students understand the systemic ways inequality is perpetuated. That it is not their fault that they are in those classes; rather, it is the result of years of racial discrimination that has demeaned Black and Latinx intelligence, that has insisted on tracking systems that consistently result in a different educational experience for them, that has created an educational system that demands restructuring and keeps their needs at the center. Resistance and how BIPOC youth and collaborators have organized against systems are also important to center.

The importance of social change—and the responsibility of all members within the community to work for that change—is embedded within CRILCs. It is a value to which educators and students return to again and again, especially during times when they might feel discouraged or disillusioned. We have many models of collectivist social change, including powerful examples of young people leading the way, that can provide us with necessary jolts of encouragement along the way. We should regularly draw on those examples for inspiration and direction. We should be especially intentional, too, of making sure all the examples our BIPOC students see are of BIPOC organizers doing the work. White students also need to see these examples so they can have an expanded understanding of solidarity and the work BIPOC young people are doing to impact social change.

To-Do's

Learn about systems of inequality within your classroom and within your school. Consult disciplinary data, Advanced Placement data, teacher racial makeup and other sources that could have disparities. Ask students where they notice unfairness, inequity, or injustice, too. Think about what patterns and systems are present and how you might work with students and other community members to challenge and change those systems. What is the next step you and your students might make as they begin to enact this change?

Takeaway

CRILCs have specific values that include being asset-based, encouraging and nurturing vulnerability, and being driven by collectivism and sociopolitical change. The values are an important part of creating a literacy community driven by action, setting the stage for the actions that occur within.

Actions of CRILCs

CRILCs have three primary umbrella actions that guide community interactions. These actions are how values are embodied in the everyday. They are what we do. The actions of CRILCs are to intentionally and consistently

- Eliminate traditional barriers to literacy;
- Address and heal reading trauma and curriculum violence;
- Deliberately teach and hand over the habits, skills, and dispositions required to be a high literacy achiever to every single student.

CRILCs eliminate traditional barriers to literacy. How much of the routines and practices of our literacy instruction are grounded in the best culturally relevant and sustaining research, especially about Black and Latinx students? Do we allow that research to guide our instruction? Do we continually reflect on and update our knowledge in response to that research? We must.

When I began teaching, I was as concerned with "accountability" as I was with finding books that young people wanted to read. I needed to know if young people were, essentially, following my directions (instead of actually reading, comprehending, and enjoying their texts). Reading logs, one-pagers that required students to record what they read daily outside class, proved detrimental to my goals of creating an intentional literacy community.

My decision to assign reading logs was not based on any sort of research that improved the literacy outcomes of readers. *None.*

"Reading log Mondays" quickly became the bane of my existence. Students would hand them in incomplete, illegible, or, as they eventually came to tell me, with forged signatures. Because they were graded, students were vulnerable. After reminding myself that my goal was to get young people to love reading and listening to my students' feedback about the assignment, it made sense to eliminate any and all barriers standing in the way of achieving that goal. Thus, reading logs had to go.

Dr. Cris Tovani (2016) challenges us to connect our practice to research. She says we should be able to affirm, "I can cite the research that informs my practice." Many of our beloved "best literacy practices" have no grounding in research. If they are research-based, that research does not always provide culturally relevant suggestions for our students because the research has not been conducted with or by researchers who reflect diverse populations.

The National Council of Teachers of English (NCTE) is a reputable source for evaluating our literacy practices. I recommend beginning with the organization's position statements, which span a range of current and enduring literacy issues (https://ncte.org/resources /position-statements/all/). If we focus on reading logs, often used as a type of assessment, NCTE's (2018a) "Literacy Assessment: Definitions, Principles and Practices" can guide us. The statement asserts, "Literacy assessment is a social process, not a technical activity," and "Literacy assessment is meaningful to the learner" (paras. 06, 08). Reading logs are neither social nor meaningful to the learner. A quick survey of your own readers' opinions on reading logs can provide some authentic, personalized data if you're still hesitant to eliminate them.

I replaced reading logs with reading conferences. Reading conferences are quick check-ins and conversations about what students were reading that enabled me to collect real-time, robust information and to make on-the-spot changes and suggestions to help young people find books that were right for them. As we go about working with our students to build intentional classroom literacy spaces, we must be mindful about the barriers that can hinder our most important work and eliminate them. Turning to research-backed literacy organizations like NCTE can help us make informed, culturally relevant decisions in the best interest of our students.

To-Do's

Consider your literacy practices throughout your career and conduct an audit about literacy barriers you have created—unintentionally or otherwise. Spend some time reflecting on research that supports your decisions while also evaluating the backgrounds of the researchers conducting the studies. Then, actively decide what barriers to eliminate from your literacy instruction, and also what new assignments and practices can support the positive growth of your students, are not punitive, and are grounded in equity and justice.

CRILCs address and heal reading trauma and curriculum violence. Curriculum violence can occur in our classrooms. Dr. Stephanie P. Jones (2020) explains, "Curriculum violence occurs when educators and curriculum writers have constructed a set of lessons that damage or otherwise adversely affect students intellectually and emotionally" (para. 07). Reading logs—and the stress, shame, and blame they can create for students and caregivers if they do not complete them—is a type of curriculum violence. Another regular practice of CRILCs is that we must work to actively and consistently heal this damage while also working diligently to prevent more from occurring.

Reading trauma is only one form of curriculum violence in ELA classrooms that has inflicted substantial harm on students. Torres and Stivers (cited in Dankowski, 2020) define *reading trauma* as "a potential source of pain, insecurity, humiliation, or stress" (para. 01). They include high-stakes testing, a fixation on the "classics," and shaming readers for their choices as some of the causes of reading trauma. We must think about the ways that our decisions create the very deficits and gaps we want our practice to remedy. If we are causing reading trauma and curriculum violence, which we can determine through auditing our curriculum and what our students have said about it (NYU's Culturally Responsive Curriculum Scorecard is a comprehensive starting place: https://steinhardt.nyu.edu/metrocenter /perspectives/introducing-culturally-responsive-curriculum-scorecard -tool-evaluate), then we must stop. Immediately.

In CRILCs, reading happens on a continuum, and, for many students, we have to determine where students' reading progress has been interrupted or changed. The educator's responsibility is to determine where and when the reading speed bumps and difficulties occurred in a student's history, first, and then actively work to heal them. For instance, if I know that readers have been shamed because they enjoy reading graphic novels, I'm going to celebrate that a young person has found a genre that resonates with them. Also, because CRILCs actively work to end curriculum violence, I will regularly audit my classroom library and the core texts I teach and have taught throughout the last few years, particularly with an eye toward representation, absences, and silences, and address those gaps by adding texts and centering what students want to read.

We cannot be willfully ignorant when we are developing our classroom libraries or making other choices about texts. If we are curating a classroom library, for instance, our own preferences should not be more important than our readers'. I am not the most avid reader of fantasy and science fiction. A classroom audit of my collection revealed that I had far fewer titles in that genre than in other genres. What I knew, though, from talking with students and reading of their surveys, was that they *loved* science fiction and fantasy. It was one of their most popular genres. I admitted to students that I'd let my own disinterest lead to not doing what they were telling me they desired. I asked them what they wanted me to add to the classroom library, as well as what texts they wanted to read during our collective work, and I changed based on that feedback. Our science fiction/fantasy section doubled, and readers were able to offer continuous feedback that enabled their literacy practices to flourish.

We also need to be aware of how we practice language acceptance within our CRILCs. Specifically, some students of African descent likely speak multiple varieties of English, including African American Vernacular English (AAVE), or Ebonics. Classrooms are not always so accepting of Black Language, unfortunately, and teachers often do not understand or value Black language.

When we condemn Black students' language—and other students who speak a broad variety of languages, too—we condemn students. We practice another form of curriculum violence, this time in linguistic form. I, too, have used the terms *Standard English*, and I, too, have taught students how to "code-switch" from AAVE to that Standard English. Because of the recent research from Dr. April Baker-Bell and the work of CCCC, I now understand the harm I've caused for so many students because I failed to thoroughly interrogate the white supremacy inherent in valuing "Standard English," which is now understood to be "White Mainstream English." I thought that I was doing enough to prepare my students of color to be in the world, but I was wrong.

Now, I am guided by Baker-Bell's insistence that we use the language of "anti-Black linguistic racism" as we understand the harm we do by asking students to divorce their identity from their language. This shift means that liberatory teachers intentionally change their practices, becoming ones who "stop promoting and privileging White Mainstream English, code-switching, and contrastive analysis at the expense of Black students. This is linguistically violent to the humanity and spirit of Black Language speakers" (CCCC, 2020, para. 14). Instead, we address the politics and racialized ways language functions, *with* students, while we simultaneously affirm the beauty and power of Black Language. The CCCC's position statement is a key place to begin challenging our own beliefs about Black Language and taking the suggested action steps to change our practice as we work toward linguistic justice for our students.

I imagine that for some educators, it might be difficult to admit mistakes to students, but I have found that regularly saying where I fell short builds trust and confidence among all of us. (I am modeling and practicing vulnerability, also). Then, I work to repair harm, something that happens over time. Also, the modeling that I do for students is powerful, and applies the CRILC principle: through addressing the reading trauma I inflict on students, and actively and intentionally working to remedy it and change my practices, we move toward collective healing.

To-Do's

Read the CCCC's "Demand for Black Linguistic Justice" (https://cccc.ncte.org/cccc/demand-for-black-linguistic-justice), paying particular attention to the expectations for teachers. What might be implications for your work with Black, Latinx, and other students of color who all speak varieties of English? How might understanding the CCCC's Demand scaffold affect your thinking about other types of curriculum violence in your literacy practices? What can you do to eliminate them and repair damage immediately?

CRILCs deliberately teach and hand over the habits, skills, and dispositions required to be a literacy high achiever. Teachers are central to developing CRILCs and explicitly expressing their purposes, goals, and outcomes. As Dr. Richard Milner (2020) explains, "Educators themselves can be seen as curriculum engineers who orchestrate and co-construct with students learning opportunities" (p. 152). Without the commitment from a teacher, it's simply impossible to realize all a CRILC can become. Even with the most committed students, without a teacher who believes in them and who champions their literacy achievement, a CRILC will be ineffective. We must be educators who value children, their rights to literacy, and their belief in creating and maintaining a CRILC.

In CRILCs, being a literacy achiever can be taught. Building on the skills that students bring into our classrooms, we as educators must identify the additional habits, dispositions, and practices that students need to master to be successful. This mastery extends beyond being able to demonstrate proficiency on necessary skills (i.e., reading comprehension, standardized testing, writing for on-demand tasks) to the higher-order work that academic scholars within academic communities take up regularly. In these communities, which CRILCs resemble in their highest forms, students engage in high-level discussions generated by their own interpretations and lived experiences that connect to what is being studied. They write in ways that respond to the worlds in which they live, to audiences that are appropriate for what they want to say.

Through a series of regular informal assessments that can take the shape of reading conferences, surveys, or low-stakes informal interviews with small groups of students, a teacher is able to get a grasp on what their students know and where to devote some strategic energy. If, for instance, an educator discerns that students need practice with a particular way that an argument can be structured based on a task (writing an open letter, for instance) after chatting with them about what they already know or even having them label what parts of the structure are familiar to them, next steps could be having students study actual mentor texts of open letters. The teacher can then move back and forth as students notice common features, identify those features, then try their hands at writing the open letter based on their expanded understanding of the task. It is in this observing, talking to students, designing tasks, then taking up a process to achieve a task that a teacher can get students on board systematically.

The classroom has a general hum of productivity that can sound different on any given day depending on the literacy tasks being undertaken. In these shared spaces, students might simultaneously be participating in a writing workshop model, drafting their writing, sharing their work with peers, or conferencing with a teacher. On other days, students might be practicing the skill of close reading with attention to diction, tone, or syntax. None of these interactions is haphazard, though. Actions, outcomes, and the overall path for mastery are understood and enacted by everyone within the community.

Planning for Success

In general, the educator draws on a range of planning tools to guide instructional practices that include the state standards and others like the Learning for Justice Social Justice Standards to assure they are addressing antibias practices at core, too. We also teach to grade-level standards consistently. I often had a matrix that covered the skills I needed to teach explicitly, through minilessons, targeted practice, and follow up until students demonstrated mastery.

Then, I thought, too, about "transfer," to use the language of Understanding by Design. More specifically, the goal of student understanding, as Wiggins and McTighe (2005) remind us, is how to make meaning of "big ideas" and transfer their learning. It's not enough for students to demonstrate competency during the study of one particular novel, for example, or on a standardized test, which we can often get fixated on if we are in high-stakes environments. Rather, we want them to be able to know how to read a text, how to make meaning from it, how to apply their own lenses, and then how to write about what they know in ways that can be applied flexibly to whatever genre and audience they are addressing. We want, and need, to teach them to transfer their learning to mastering other tasks.

The educator also tracks mastery and transfer for all students, knowing that students will demonstrate competence and mastery at different rates, but the goal is that all students reach that point. Mastery and transfer are expected and explicitly taught. Importantly, the educator makes mastery and goals clear to all students so they know the expectations, too. Thus, the nature of CRILCs is recursive, looping back to provide reinforcement for those who need more time, while also extending opportunities for those who are ready for the next challenge. Providing challenge, especially for BIPOC students, is also important so they can always be realizing and stretching beyond their limits. In CRILCs, though, mastery occurs on a continuum, with plenty of time and space for practicing the habits and skills needed to keep making progress.

It's worthwhile to address concerns about students who are "behind" or "not making adequate progress," as we often label students who are not at the same level of academic achievement as determined by grade-level specifics. We must first figure out how "behind" these students are and what is the root cause. We should start with our students, genuinely curious about what they tell us and how that can help us to work with them to move them ahead. We also need to lean on being expansive in our thinking about where we want students to go and what mastery looks like. Mastery must be culturally relevant, too, and also expected and taught for all of our students, even ones who will need additional time to get there. We don't give up on them.

Failure and Growth

CRILCs reject all deficit language and theories (of "gaps" and "learning loss," especially). Because this harmful language is so pervasive, it's important to continually examine the ways we have internalized deficit language in our practices and by our students, and work to challenge and eliminate that language. Dr. Theresa Perry's

(Perry, Steele, & Hilliard, 2003) notion of counternarratives frames our thinking about why we must be deliberate about making CRILCs spaces where counternarratives are about achievement, and, in this case, particularly about the achievement of African American youth. Perry writes:

> Even if education leads to a good job, even if African-American parents communicate clearly to their children that education pays off, these experiences can be neutralized if children experience school and the larger society as unfair and discriminatory. In other words, a child's belief in the power and importance of schooling and intellectual work can be interrupted by teachers and others who explicitly or subtly convey a disbelief in the child's ability for high academic achievement, and the child having a rightful place in the larger society—unless a counternarrative about the child's identity as an intellectual being is intentionally passed on to him or her. (p. 79)

This insistence on seeing students as intellectual beings, especially ones who are Black, Latinx, Indigenous, and other POCs, is another deliberate aim of CRILCs. The first step of this insistence is understanding the many ways intellectuals populate communities already. They exist beyond academe. Intellectuals, and intellectual traditions, are everywhere: they are educators, yes, and are also parents, store owners, neighbors. Engaging students in a community-mapping exercise can help to reinforce these understandings, as will a broader conversation about knowledge and how much of what we can think and believe about being "smart" is based on white supremacy. We can work with students to change our understanding of intelligence. We can also draw on history for rich examples and inspiration for our students, especially ways Black people and others practiced literacy despite threat of death. Then, we need to document those examples in our classrooms so students always know.

Helpful, too, is the work of Carol Dweck (2006) and growth mindset. I regularly repeated Dweck's reminder that "smart is not what you are—smart is what you get" to students, regardless of what work we did. So many carried stories of failure, and had not had ample opportunity to process those moments and to also contextualize them within a broader continuum of learning. Failure happens; however, if we can process and learn from those failures through regular reflection, failure can be viewed as necessary to any progress we hope to make. For BIPOC students, though, this attention to failure *and* success can be absent, causing them to blame themselves.

I learned that moving students past their literacy failures was also critical, as many had internalized that they were always going to dislike reading or felt reading was something they simply couldn't "do." An effective assignment for setting the tone of how to address failure as a part of learning is the literacy failure narrative. I found that spending time early in the year writing failure narratives—a short writing assignment that asked them to identify a moment in their reading lives where they felt unsuccessful—was important in helping me figure out what harm they carried with them and also in helping me create an environment of acknowledging failures and what we learned from those experiences. I, too, wrote a short narrative and workshopped it with students to model my own failures and what I continue to learn.

The process of reflecting on the failure was paramount. When students were able to reframe the experience, they could begin to understand that, though significant, those moments were not how students had to continually define themselves. When we shared those narratives, we created a foundation for community that accomplished several goals. First, it helped to begin developing shared language for how to talk about achievement and failure. Second, it let students know how much they had in common and that they were not alone or different or guilty for failing. Finally, the failure narratives was a low-stakes writing assignment that enabled me to introduce structures and processes for the writing workshop that organized our instructional time.

Structured Spaces

Writing workshops are also an example of a component of CRILCs that honor structure and automaticity, consistent actions that support students' success. CRILCs are, indeed, structured spaces when it comes to routines and rituals. Often, activities happen at the same time, every day. For instance, my classes always begin with 20 minutes of daily independent reading time. I spend the early part of our year acclimating students to the expectations of the ritual. After establishing community agreements together, I guide students through a discussion of why classes begin with reading: that in order to develop or sustain a reading habit, they must have time to read and practice becoming proficient. They need to have the time and space also to conference with me about their reading so I can track their progress, make sure they are regularly challenging themselves as readers, and learn how I can help them should they get stuck. Reading in community is powerful. I do not expect them to simply jump right into these practices, though. Until they demonstrate mastery, practicing the routines *is* the curriculum.

My goal is to ingrain particular practices as automatic. If reading is so consistent, if it happens at the same time daily, and if the expectations are always the same, then students know what is expected and are more likely to do it. They are also able to teach new members who join the community. Moreover, if I explicitly and regularly reinforce those structures and routines, students are more likely to internalize those practices for themselves. What I've also found is that students often become so accustomed to reading for a particular time each day that they continue this practice once our time together ends. Other routines and structures that are important to teach to students include participating in various types of discussions, addressing feedback, working collaboratively in groups, and completing homework.

Homework is another element that supports structure and automaticity in CRILCs. The goal of homework is for students to practice a skill as they work toward mastery. Homework is not a time for students to attempt unfamiliar concepts without my assistance; rather, it's a time to reinforce habits and consistent, intentional practice. Students are always assigned an additional 20 minutes of nightly reading for homework. Even though I stopped assigning reading logs to track their progress, I am still able to know if students are completing their reading through asking them during reading conferences or some other time.

The process for creating any classroom structure is generally the same. First, a teacher needs to determine the necessity for a productive routine. Thinking about how it would benefit a CRILC and how receptive students might be to its incorporation helps if that structure or routine is essential. In the case of nightly reading homework, we want students to practice their reading. We also want them to develop a reading habit. It makes sense to assign that homework, to check in about the homework, and to help them troubleshoot when and if they don't complete that homework consistently. These steps should not be punitive. Instead, they should be holistic and reflective, seeking to determine ways to develop and cultivate a habit that we want to become automatic.

To-Do's

What habits, skills, and dispositions do students need explicit instruction in learning? Think about "hidden curriculum," especially, defined as "the unspoken or implicit academic, social, and cultural messages that are communicated to students while they are in school" (Ed Glossary, 2015), and which parts of that hidden curriculum can be made explicit to benefit BIPOC students (how to talk to a teacher about requesting a revision of a paper, for instance). Craft a matrix of those skills and dispositions, then add standards to determine where there is potential for synthesizing those skills and standards for designing curricular lessons.

Takeaway

Culturally relevant intentional literacy communities are places that encourage a deep, sustained engagement with young people around transformative literacy practices and beliefs. Through purposeful values and actions, it is possible for a teacher to engineer and collaboratively establish classrooms as spaces that repair harm and create expectations and practices with students that make normalizing their high achievement paramount. In the next chapter, I look specifically at routines and traditions that support and encourage the daily values of CRILCs that teachers can implement immediately with their students.

Routines and Traditions
of CRILCs

What can we do now, to create a world we want to live in?
—*Octavia Butler*

Community building takes practice and participation that a teacher facilitates through meaningful, culturally relevant and affirming routines, rituals, and traditions. The objective for this chapter is to describe the routines and traditions of CRILCs; consider why routines and traditions are important, then look at a few specific ones of CRILCs.

Defining Routines and Traditions

Culturally relevant routines and traditions create and sustain connections within CRILCs. By centering student choice and agency, they seek to establish a counternarrative about achievement for Black,

Latinx, and other POC youth. These intentional actions help children realize their "identity as intellectual beings" (Perry et al., 2003, p. 79). Routines and traditions enable us to support the identity development of our BIPOC students.

Routines are ways of being and acting that enable us to function. My life runs on routines: I get up, have my coffee, and go running most mornings, for example. My small habits build the routine. Then, when I'm out for my run, I'm able to do some of my best thinking because my mind is relatively uncluttered, because I've followed the routine. I'm able to do the work I really want and need to do. The goal of this teaching is that our routines become so normalized that students do them without fuss. They simply become the way we do things.

The routines and structures we want to implement require lots of practice, reinforcement, and troubleshooting before they become automatic. Also, as with any routine, they need revisiting as students develop their familiarity. Routines are never punitive; rather, because they are a structured part of the CRILCs, we practice them with students for as long as is required.

Traditions enable cultures and beliefs to be communicated and handed over to those within a community. Practicing and upholding traditions has many benefits: members learn important history, are affirmed as part of that community, and solidify their relationships and connections with others inside that community. Traditions can also be celebratory, used to mark important moments in time, to note accomplishments, and to remind those within a community about a shared purpose. In CRILCs, traditions aim to solidify students' positive reading identities and reading development.

CRILCs have specific values and actions. They are grounded in routines and traditions that permeate all aspects of the classroom and to which teachers and students return to again and again. Routines reinforce ways of being, communicate an unfailing belief in the power and promise of the children within it, and function as types of texts. In this chapter, I focus on four powerful routines and traditions that support a culturally relevant literacy classroom: independent choice reading, reading conferences, classroom libraries, and "Literary Citizens of the World."

Independent Choice Reading as Routine

Everyone deserves the freedom to read whatever they want to read. They also need the freedom to *not* read or to abandon what they're reading (see the National Council of Teachers of English [2018] position statement "The Students' Right to Read" for more). Unfortunately, BIPOC students often don't have those freedoms. If they are in low-performing schools, they are more likely to have "drill-and-kill," excerpted reading aimed at increasing their performance on standardized tests. They also have most likely read texts that have not reflected or affirmed their broad backgrounds. Students in these contexts are most likely to benefit from a robust literacy experience, but they are unlikely to experience that benefit because of the other demands schooling places on them.

What we need is a reframing of how choice and independent reading act as a routine for anchoring students in literacy and supporting students' development of a love of literacy.

We know that reading proficiency is tied to all sorts of successes. The challenge, though, is too many students have had few opportunities to be immersed in a classroom literacy culture that centers their entire reading development. If students have not gained grade-level proficiency, their time is mostly taken up in remediation. It is often during these moments (and even years) of focused instruction that young people tell me they experienced a significant disconnect in their personal reading identities because the tasks did nothing to develop an understanding of the broader goals of liberatory literacy and competence. Reading became something that was unpleasurable, a chore, or something they could not "get" or "do."

However, students do not develop these negative experiences on their own. They are in classrooms where seldom, if ever, are they asked what matters to them and to their reading lives. When we listen to our students, they'll tell us, over and over again, that they want to decide what they want to read.

Independent reading offers tremendous promise for changing the lives of young people. The National Council of Teachers of English (2019c) defines independent reading as follows:

> Independent reading is a routine, protected instructional practice that occurs across all grade levels. Effective independent reading practices include **time** for students to read, **access** to books that represent a wide range of characters and experiences, and **support** within a reading community that includes teachers and students. Student choice in text is essential because it motivates, engages, and reaches a wide variety of readers. **The goal of independent reading as an instructional practice is to build habitual readers with conscious reading identities.** (para. 02; boldface mine)

We adults know that if we are allowed to choose what we want to read, we are much more likely to actually read something. Our students are no different.

Steps to Introduce an Independent Reading Routine

1. Decide what are the critical elements of a routine. Walk through it in your mind from start to finish. What would need to happen to have students execute that routine proficiently? Write down those steps. They will become the subject of your minilessons as you teach students the routine.

2. Introduce the routine to students, being sure to foreground the authentic *why* of it. Ask them for their feedback and make any necessary adjustments based on their feedback.

3. Teach a series of minilessons that helps students understand the routine. Teachers can consider the following sequence of lessons for independent reading:

   a. Introduce independent reading and why daily reading in class matters and the overall importance of having a reading life.

   b. Generate a starter list of definitions for the routine. Facilitate a discussion about what a structured amount of time might look like (i.e., people reading, conferencing, or looking for a book), or sound like (minimal talking; short, purposeful conversations between teachers and students or peers; generally quiet in the classroom). Review and update routines regularly.

   c. Discuss the purpose, function, and arrangement of classroom library or choice text selection.

   d. Explain and model how to select a book and begin reading.

   e. Describe and practice what to do if a book "isn't working."

   f. Discuss how to end independent reading time.

While it might be challenging to decide to create space in our classrooms for consistent independent reading, we must remember that this routine has tremendous capability to change the reading lives of the students most in need and deserving of fulfilling reading lives. These steps suggest a progression for introducing independent reading as a routine through a series of minilessons. These minilessons should be taught at the beginning of the time, lasting between 5 and 20 minutes. The time students have to read can increase in length as students become acclimated to the practice. Generally, starting with shorter times gives students opportunities to practice, troubleshoot, and build momentum.

It is a process, though, that has substantial impacts on our students. I conclude this section with an excerpt of a reflection from one of those young people. Ze'Voun, a Black boy in the 10th grade, who began our time together as a reader detached from his previous love of reading. Because of the ritual of daily independent reading, he regained that love. Ze'Voun had this positive association with literacy all along. I merely enacted the ritual that enabled his reconnection. Ze'Voun wrote:

> Choice in reading matters to me because I'll read more if I can choose.... Now that I have more choice as a reader and the fact that I like reading more now makes me want to strive to be an even better reader. I sometimes complain about big books but I look at them as a challenge now. I would hate to be given a book that doesn't challenge me to be a better reader. I feel like books are like clothes—everyone has a different style. Making someone read a book is almost like making them wear uniforms. Not everyone is going to like them. All these years my love for reading has been suppressed because I didn't have a choice. Now that I do have a choice I think it would kill me to go back to being assigned books. This year being able to pick the books and also being able to stop reading them if I wanted made me fall in love with reading. I actually go home and read my books because I want to.

Ze'Voun experienced significant changes to his feelings about reading and to his reading identity, and those changes were largely influenced by the consistent ritual of daily independent choice reading. For Black, Latinx, and other POC students, being deeply embedded in this routine creates the intentional setting and practice that supports their reading growth, reconnections, and change, and teachers can make it happen, daily, in their classrooms.

Takeaway

Culturally relevant routines and traditions create structures that establish and sustain community. We cannot expect our students to develop a love of reading without our support, especially those who have experienced reading trauma. Deciding to implement daily, independent reading that enables students to choose books of interest to them, read them within a classroom community, and have a teacher's support enables students to develop their positive reading identities.

To-Do's

- Look closely at your daily and weekly classroom schedules. Where can you carve out consistent, daily time for independent reading? Even if you cannot initially commit to the recommended 20–30 minutes, where could you start with 10–15 minutes and then increase that time steadily?

- Survey your readers to determine their reading interests. After you review the survey results, what themes do you notice for the genres, topics, and titles that resonate with your students? What do you need to do to build your own knowledge of culturally relevant authors and illustrators working in those genres so you can help students know about them?

- Plan minilessons to introduce independent reading to students. These short lessons that anchor the independent reading time can include why it's important to take time to read and the reason for it happening in your classroom, how to select a book, how to abandon a book, and so forth. Teach these minilessons daily, while also checking in with students to determine areas of confusion and reinforcement. Using their feedback and your own observations, design additional minilessons that respond to their needs.

- Finally, make sure you are finding your own time to read texts of interest to you. We must model the love of reading for our students, talk about our reading lives with them, and be the reading representatives who can encourage and support them.

Reading Conferences as Routine

A successful independent choice reading routine is supported by reading conferences. As a way of framing this understanding, recall what NCTE (2019c) says about independent reading: "During independent reading, students spend time authentically practicing a wide variety of skills within their self-selected books. Through practice, and with teacher support, students are able to gain the skills necessary to access a wide variety of genres and book formats" (para. 04). Reading conferences are a regular routine in a CRILC that enables a teacher to determine the progress their students are making, areas of challenge, and next steps. These brief, ongoing conversations with students happen during daily choice independent reading time. They are not optional, and they provide the additional level of teacher support students need to grow, especially regarding reading stamina, reading comprehension, and the overall joy and love of reading.

Reading conferences are a routine that students are taught. After the introduction of independent reading time and once a habit has begun to be established, teachers can then introduce reading conferences through a series of anchor minilessons. These minilessons include establishing the purpose of reading conferences (to determine how students are experiencing reading and to support their reading development), breaking down the steps of the conferences, and conducting a few reading conferences and debriefing them with the whole class. I've shown a short one- to two-minute clip of past reading conferences to introduce the expectations and used that as a point of discussion for students, probing them about what they saw the reader doing and what they saw me doing. The goal of these minilessons is to create buy-in with students, to be transparent about why reading conferences are a routine, and to clear up any potential areas of confusion.

By sitting beside them during independent reading time and asking a simple query (e.g., "Tell me about what's going on in your reading, please"), a teacher gets a rich window into a reader's experience and steps for how to address what that reader needs. This low-stakes invitation is the start of the routine.

From the reader's response, a teacher can glean information for next steps. If a reader seems to be enjoying their book, the teacher can probe for details to determine if the student understands what they are reading, and to what degree (i.e., a formative assessment for reading comprehension). If a reader seems stuck or disinterested, the teacher can then dig into potential reasons: Lack of interest in the topic? Not the right match with reading level, perhaps? A teacher needs to stop the reading conference immediately to address the problem the reader is having once they've come to some initial hunches. I've often gathered a stack of potential titles for a reader who has had difficulty finding a book they like, either quickly previewing those books as I put them on their desk or simply laying out some books I think might resonate with a reader.

Reading conferences are a foundational part of a CRILC because they provide real-time data about the work we need to do to support and extend our students' reading development. Again, these conferences need not be long—just long enough to connect with a student, extract information from the reader, and determine next steps for both teacher and student. Also, a goal teachers can set is to have a reading conference with every student a predetermined number of times per semester or grading period and work their way down the roster. Of course, students who are struggling take precedence. If a student needs help finding a book, is changing books frequently, or is not reading at all, then the teacher should attend to that student immediately, then return to the rest of their roster. See Figure 4.1 for more tips on conducting a reading conference. For stuck readers, we can't wait for them to figure out why they aren't reading. We have to jump in and help.

Takeaway

Reading conferences are a routine that enables teachers to get to know their students as readers, to continue to move them along in their reading development, and to sustain the overall goal of connecting with students and their literacy needs. They happen regularly, with the intention of the teacher always knowing how students are doing and how to assist them as readers.

To-Do's

Practice having a reading conference with students, taking notes along the way to have for future reference. Reflect on the process, especially what you learn about your students as readers. Ask them also to reflect on the process and debrief together, with the goal of incorporating reading conferences as a classroom routine. Consider how you will hold yourself accountable for achieving your goals.

FIGURE 4.1

How to Have a Reading Conference

1. **Decide when reading conferences will happen**. During daily independent reading time is usually an ideal time.

2. **Prepare students**. Let them know what a reading conference is about and the purpose. Reassure students that they are not punitive but, rather, a way for teachers to get to know who they are as readers. Tell students, too, that during these short chats, you'll be asking them questions about their book, what they're going to read next, or about any focused minilessons you're following up on.

3. **Gather your materials**. A binder or notebook with a page for every student will enable taking notes as you talk to students. There are also apps (e.g., Evernote) that can make this record keeping easier.

4. **Start your reading conferences**. Have a general low-stakes question to start your conferences (e.g., "Can you tell me about what you're reading?"), and really listen to what students say. Sit beside them, as it's often easier for students to talk to teachers shoulder-to-shoulder rather than eye-to-eye. You might have a list of probes that help you determine whether students are understanding what they are reading, other probes to determine whether they are challenging themselves, or more general probes to cover a range of topics. Keep these pasted in your binder or notebook so you can access them easily throughout your conferences. Take notes about readers as you go, as these notes provide rich information about students' growth and challenges.

5. **Take action; solve problems**. Students might reveal that they are not reading their current book (or the teacher figures that out) or that they are not enjoying their book. There's no time to wait when this occurs. Stop the conference and help the student find something else to read. Pull a range of books from the classroom library and help the reader peruse potential new choices. Readers need teachers to help them get unstuck and to normalize the need to find texts that match where they are at the moment, without any shame or blame.

6. **Conference with every student**. Work down your roster, with the goal of seeing every student for a conference. Then, start over. If students are in distress, though (i.e., not reading, or having a difficult time finding something to read), move those students to the top of the roster and help them first before returning to the rest of the order.

Classroom Libraries as Tradition

What might it mean to envision and enact humanizing, liberatory classrooms that are made especially for BIPOC students? Classroom libraries have an important role. We can create them to be sites of freedom, extending and deepening our intentional, foundational work.

In its position statement about the importance of classroom libraries, NCTE (2021) explains that they "offer ongoing opportunities for teachers to work with students as individuals to find books that will ignite their love for learning, calm their fears, answer their questions, and improve their lives in any of the multiple ways that only literature can" (n.p.). Essentially, by providing our readers with a range of texts from which they can choose, that reflect their interests, and that encourage them to expand their horizons through a classroom library, we are being liberatory practitioners.

I've always had a classroom library. I didn't even realize it was a tradition until I overheard students talking to their peers about it, about the texts within it, about the freedom they had to read whatever they wanted, and about how they often stopped back in to see what had been added to it. The tradition of the classroom library meant that students used it as a means of practicing their literacy. It was a tangible indicator of the possibilities that could support their reading lives. The tradition was that new students would inherit the library at the start of a new school year and then become stewards of that library when they joined the community.

In the early days of teaching, my libraries were a random collection of books I gathered from Goodwill stores, yard sales, and donations. The majority did not reflect the identities of the Black and Latinx students I taught. However, I now think it was some combination of simply being surrounded by so many books (bookcases were everywhere; it seemed books were always either falling off shelves or stacked haphazardly from where students sifted through to find something to read), coupled with an expectation that they would find *something* on those shelves that spoke to them and I would be relentless to make reading matches, that compelled so many of my young people to read. I also was explicit about my expectation that they read daily, in class, for at least 20 minutes.

As I learned more about the importance of cultivating a library that reflected students' interests, I refined my classroom library using information I regularly gained through reading conferences and informal conversations with my students. Knowing that students were keenly interested in science fiction and fantasy, I had a substantial section of the library dedicated to that genre. Then, within science fiction and fantasy, I looked for titles that reflected #Own Voices (Duyvis, 2015) and BIPOC authors. Frequently, the classroom library was the first place readers were exposed to texts written by authors who shared their racial and ethnic backgrounds. Other sections I built out after listening to students included nonfiction about sports, war, and other specific topics they requested or expressed interest in learning more about.

I enlisted students to help in the upkeep of the classroom library. They organized, alphabetized as best they could, and reshelved. I wanted them to know that the books belonged to all of us. Limiting their interactions with the books would have been a barrier. Instead, I did spend some time teaching them about how they could return or check out books (I used the Booksource system to manage check-ins and returns), how to make recommendations for books they thought we should add to the library (index cards located in a consistent area of the classroom that I consulted regularly), and how to be responsible community members when it came to library maintenance (i.e., keeping the library tidy and taking care of books). These short lessons were embedded in overall instructional time, often buttressing daily reading time, and posed as gentle reminders and lessons about how to keep the classroom library functioning for the overall enjoyment of everyone.

Takeaway

Classroom libraries are important for connecting students to reading. With thoughtful introductions and use, students have powerful ways of building their reader identities, of strengthening community connections, and of understanding why the right to read and to have access to texts is something they deserve wherever they go.

To-Do's

- Decide to create a classroom library, regardless of the grade level or subject you teach. If you are a subject-area teacher, think about what range of texts relate to your subject that can appeal to a range of students. Think broadly about texts and genres, including graphic novels, poetry, and picture books. Also, consider how you can enlist the support and expertise of your school or community librarian.

- If you already have a classroom library, audit it to determine how culturally relevant and reflective of your students' broad experiences the library is. Using Learning for Justice's Reading Diversity tool (https://www.tolerance .org/magazine/publications/reading-diversity), reflect on the results and make necessary changes to assure your library is culturally relevant. Those changes might include removing or adding texts. This audit is a powerful opportunity to include students in these decisions as well, increasing their ownership of the routines and their reading lives.

- Consider potential sources for books. I've had success with creating wish lists for family and friends that enable them to purchase books for my classroom from my local Black-owned independent bookstore. Other teachers have used First Book to purchase texts as well as advanced reader's copies (ARCs) of texts to populate their libraries. The goal is to have a robust collection that is reflective of readers' interests and aspirations that can expand throughout the year.

"Literary Citizens of the World" as Tradition

Dr. Nancy Tolson (2021) addresses the long history of Black children's literature: "We are permanently a part of U.S. literature" (n.p.). BIPOCs have a robust history of literary achievement. Even during the COVID-19 pandemic, BIPOC authors, illustrators, and poets have continued to create, offering their excellence and opening their studios to perform readings, to participate in panels, and to buoy educators' and students' spirits. Dr. Nancy Tolson (2021) addresses the long history of Black children's literature being more than 100 years old, saying, "We are permanently a part of U.S. literature" (n.p.). Young people need to know they belong to this literary history, and they are responsible for its continuance. However, if they do not have access to a broad literary experience that connects them to past and present, they will be unable to assure that continuity. Black, Latinx, and other POC students also need ample opportunities to experience and share literary moments to know who they can become, too. There is no more powerful way to understand and make real those possibilities than meeting an author or illustrator in person.

I live in Boston, a city with a rich literary history and an active literary culture. Readings and performances are ongoing, often featuring

BIPOC authors. However, those spaces can be unwelcoming for BIPOC youth when they are held at bookstores in non-BIPOC communities or are in places that are unwilling to understand and accept how BIPOC children and young people can show up in spaces (boisterous, full of energy and life), making the experience uncomfortable for our students.

BIPOC youth deserve to take up all the literary space they desire, including literary public spaces. Because I have long viewed my classroom as extending beyond our walls, it was logical for me to consider how I could embrace Boston's literary traditions as an extension of our classroom in ways that built on our intentional literacy community. I created "Literary Citizens of the World" (LCOTW) as a way to normalize the practice of attending literary events and to make that practice an enjoyable tradition that young people would continue after our time together concluded. As LCOTW, I rationalized that we would attend lectures by authors we might have never known, enter spaces we didn't know existed, support Black- and POC-owned venues to recognize and affirm our local communities, and continue to think about ideas generated from those outings as part of our responsibility for being in this world.

At the start of every year, I introduced LCOTW as a way for young people to take ownership of their literacy. I curated a calendar of local events, often held at bookstores and libraries, that I thought would be interesting to them; for example, the author shared one of their identities, or the event helped extend or synthesize something we were, or would be, studying. I was diligent about always including authors and illustrators that shared their backgrounds. If I had copies of the literature, I featured it prominently in the classroom library, read aloud from it on occasion, and encouraged students to explore it to build familiarity and excitement for the author.

I often attended those events myself and used the bridge of time between the end of school and the start of a reading for informal community building with students. I credit those unstructured moments as gifts for me to learn more about who they were as young people in the world: their interests, their dreams, their challenges. I was also able to spend time chatting about books and writing, finding that young people who were reticent in class were often more willing to tell me what was on their mind when the day officially ended.

Prior to the event, we selected a place to eat (usually pizza), then walked to the bookstore. If in Harvard Square, where most of the readings were, we also spent time browsing through the bookstore. In the past, I've been able to work with schools and bookstores to provide money for students to select a book or two of their own, which has sometimes been the featured book of the reading and, at other times, a book of their choice. Plenty of times, I've needed to speak to staff, employees, and others about their inappropriate policing of BIPOC young people, often while white young people are in the space doing the same thing. (These moments also become important and necessary fodder for debriefing the experience as a point of helping young people develop their sociopolitical consciousness.)

We experience the event together. We sit together, we witness the readings together, and we debrief the next day in class together. The groups that attend these events range in size, from nearly an entire class to a handful of students, and since they are generally after school, they are always voluntary. I always build in time to chat about the experience, letting those who attended share their impressions while also maintaining a supportive environment that encourages those who didn't attend but might be able to in the future. We talk about why we need to be in these spaces and what factors and systems have prevented access for BIPOC folks. We talk about what authors have said that resonate with us. We turn over our questions. We show our autographed books to each other. We invite others to join us for the next time. The goal is that there is always a next time, whether we will be together or on our own. Eventually, students shoulder more of the work of finding and suggesting events. They bring in announcements from the newspaper, read from Instagram or other news from social media, and invite the classroom community to events they think would qualify for LCOTW. When this moment happens, it's powerful, as students have assumed responsibility for helping the greater community. They have become the literary citizens of the world we need them to become.

Takeaway

The excitement that students carry with them from the LCOTW experiences linger, especially if the presenter was a young adult author (e.g., Angie Thomas). The goal of LCOTW is for young people to extend and to connect their literacy experiences to spaces outside classrooms, allowing them to see that literacies are everywhere and that they are entitled to enjoying and experiencing them. If we are intentional about creating these moments for young people, we can see LCOTW as another piece of building and sustaining a strong literacy community for BIPOC and other youth. We can celebrate literacy in external spaces, using those experiences as a thoughtful bridge to connect with our students and let them see the possibilities and necessity for enjoying this tradition.

To-Do's

Where are the spaces in your community that offer author appearances that might appeal to your students? Be intentional about exploring Black, Latinx, and POC bookstores in advance. Spend some time curating a potential calendar and share it with your students. Ask for their feedback. Aim for representing a range of voices, especially from Black, Latinx, POC, queer, and other literary talents. Then, attend a reading with your students!

- Get to know what literary history exists in the communities where your students reside. If there are historical sites that honor BIPOC authors and illustrators, see if it's possible to visit those places or to invite an expert to visit your classroom (either in person or via videoconference) to help students understand the rich histories they inherit and should know.

- Document all the ways students take up becoming Literary Citizens of the World. Consider enlisting them to create digital archives that can be shared with families and the broader community about the authors and illustrators students meet, the history they learn, and what else they discover along the way. Let them know that they are part of a tradition and that you expect them to participate and continue.

Evolving Throughout the Year: Next Steps

After committing to making classrooms intentional literacy spaces, the work takes shape differently as the school year progresses. Building a collaborative relationship with your students is imperative. But what happens next?

Continuing to deepen your understanding about your students is important. You'll learn about them through conversations in class, through observations about their interactions with their peers, through check-ins with their families if you are interested in really getting to know and, ideally, *love* them. Use this information to challenge, affirm, and extend who your students are and what they need; anticipate when you'll need to introduce them to particular authors and experiences through texts and assignments. Remember, the goal is to have a complex, multistranded understanding of who they are—a 360 understanding, if you will.

Throughout the year, teachers have ample opportunities to center, and teach from, students' interests. If we are, indeed, listening to what students are saying to us (and what they are not saying), and if we are also paying attention to the world as it presents events that demand study, then we can continue to rely on the traditions and routines that deepen our work. Because we have created this community with our students, we can make sure we are attuned to its health and long-term flourishing.

Routines can get stale, too. I conduct regular whole-class meetings to reflect on what's working within our community and what needs updating and eliminating. If something is getting on my nerves (and it's often about the care and keeping of materials), I first make sure I've spent enough time and attention teaching the routines and seeing if students are invested in learning them. If I have, then I use those meetings to understand what I'm missing and to enlist students to problem solve with me. This class meeting is never wasted time. If I've been thoughtful about creating the classroom community with my students, they will be as thoughtful and honest about helping figure out what to do next.

Traditions also need revisiting and updating. The more cohesive the classroom is, the more welcoming to new traditions it will become. Students will find ways of doing things that resonate with their entire selves. Over the years, my students have created traditions about how we began a new unit, how we made recommendations about books to read or assignments to consider, and how to settle into writing. I didn't have any ideas about those traditions before they began, honestly; I listened to my students, about how they grew into the space, how they made it their own, how they felt comfortable enough and welcomed enough to begin making their own traditions in our shared community. It is generally when students come back to see me that they articulate how those traditions made them feel seen and connected, and how the experiences were central to their positive literacy identities.

Takeaway

Routines, rituals, and traditions help us establish positive conditions for our students to succeed in our literacy classrooms. They are responsive to our students and grow and change as our students do. Now, we go deeper, thinking about how to engage with our students in discussion and interactions that are equitable and productive, the focus of the next chapter.

To-Do's

Think about how you can build on the work you're doing, or have been doing, in your classroom. What practices, routines, and traditions need refreshing or replacing? What do your students think? How can you make reflection and change a regular part of your practice? How can you hold yourself accountable, and how can you enlist your students to help keep you and themselves accountable?

5

Preparing for and Succeeding in Conversations and Interactions in CRILCs

When day comes we step out of the shade,
aflame and unafraid
The new dawn blooms as we free it
For there is always light,
if only we're brave enough to see it
If only we're brave enough to be it.
—Amanda Gorman, "The Hill We Climb"

We've spent the previous chapters establishing the importance of creating culturally relevant intentional literacy communities for students and the importance of a teacher who holds powerful beliefs in the literacy lives their students deserve. Now, we zoom into what happens in the everyday. Just because we have committed to diverse libraries and to the routines and traditions of CRILCs doesn't mean we're done. Instead, the routines and traditions are one part of the equation. What we do with those texts—our instructional practices—is critically important. In this chapter, we'll focus on moving ourselves to action through engaging in critical conversations and disrupting our curriculum.

First: What's Not OK

I was often the single Black student in classrooms where we read books with narrowly defined Black characters. There are many similar stories and experiences of limited representation that Black, Latinx, and other POC adults carry as we remember our times in school. There are stories happening, right now, to young people as you read this book. It's not the responsibility of our BIPOC students to carry the weight of explaining, testifying, or validating the educator's choices of texts. As we make decisions about curriculum, we should hold BIPOC students at the center and be able to empower them with our choices rather than harm them by committing more curriculum violence.

We must ask ourselves questions about what kinds of experiences we want all students—and especially BIPOC ones—to have when they are in our care. Do we want them to be whole and free from trauma when they leave us, having read texts that help them to understand the power of literature and their own capabilities? Or, do we want them to leave us with scars and damage from having had to endure classroom discussions and readings of texts that have made them feel humiliated, hated, and unwelcome because of our curricular choices?

Diversity, equity, and inclusion expert Erica Pernell (2020) cautions, "Talking about race in predominantly white spaces can be traumatic, painful, and harmful for BIPOC students, and there are best practices we can employ to reduce harm and provide empowering experiences" (para. 01). She recommends "avoiding simple debates," being prepared as facilitators, and building strong relationships with BIPOC students as suggestions for how to proceed with care.

If we are serious about our goal—to create and sustain a culturally relevant intentional literacy community—we must make intentional decisions about the texts we teach and how to teach them to avoid harming our students. We must give them the literacy tools to thrive as powerful readers and writers. We must choose, and deliberately enact, a different way to teach.

Creating the Foundation for Conversations

I use the language of Learning for Justice (LFJ) to describe "critical conversations" that teaching diverse texts can make possible if we are prepared to lead them with students. However, those dialogues and interactions can only be authentic and productive if we spend the time developing trusting relationships with our students. I've regularly relied on two resources: Learning for Justice's *Let's Talk* (2019) and Glenn Singleton's four agreements from his Courageous Conversations About Race (2021).

I appreciate LFJ's reframing of discussions about race, racism, white supremacy, and other potentially contentious topics as critical conversations rather than "challenging" or "uncomfortable" ones. Our language choices matter: If we set ourselves up for talking about topics that might increase our personal discomfort, we begin from a place of anxiety and worry. We can easily avoid those topics and texts, too, because of those perceived challenges, never even broaching the important conversations we should be having.

Instead, if we regard our discussions as critical and necessary, we enter them with a different connotation: that if we are willing, we can—and must—lead our students through these necessary conversations. Also, these exchanges are ongoing: they are not limited to just one text or just one moment. Even if a talk doesn't go as planned, we will most likely have another opportunity if we stay open to learning and improving how we engage. Because we are committed to culturally relevant teaching and community, these conversations must happen regularly. It is because of this regularity, too, that developing substantive relationships with our students is fundamental. Just begin.

Preparing Yourself

Chad Everett (2018), educator and equity expert, offers some insight about the necessity of having more than a commitment to diverse books in our classrooms. He says, "You can have a variety of races, abilities, gender identities, etc. represented on your shelves and still be racist, prejudiced, or homophobic in your practice and the way in which you live your life. If we stop at the presence of diverse literature on our shelves, we have missed the point" (para. 5). We must have an active commitment to having diverse, antiracist, and liberatory lives, too.

After the display of white nationalist rage during the siege on the Capitol in January 2021, many white people expressed a disconcerting amount of shock and outrage about what they deemed as "unexpected" behavior. Many of us who are Black, Latinx, and POC were not alarmed; instead, what happened confirmed what we know and live through daily (and what our students do, too): that white supremacy is alive and well and it functions through people and systems. Author Katilyn Greenidge (2021) offered, "It is America if you know any history deeper than the United States' greatest hits." Later, she noted, "I was struck, again, by the ways we are living in a story so many of us refuse to actually read" (para. 06). For white teachers, especially, that means reckoning with white racial identity, history, and how that identity affects teaching practices.

One of the pillars of culturally relevant practice is that educators develop their own cultural competence. According to administrator George Farmer (2020), "For individuals to become competent in another culture, they must first understand their own biases and stereotypical ideas. This recognition allows people to become more aware of their thoughts and actions towards others who do not look like them" (para. 08). Farmer and Ladson-Billings demand that we understand our identities and our behaviors. If our behaviors are not culturally relevant, we must interrogate our beliefs—*all* of them— and make necessary changes because we are otherwise harming our students.

Educator Sheldon Eakins (2020) talks about the work teachers can do with white students. However, his advice is relevant to the work white teachers need to do for themselves as a way of interrogating their own beliefs and biases. He says:

> It's not uncommon for White people to say, *Oh, I'm just White. I don't have a culture.* We need to teach our White students about what their cultural background is and their ethnic backgrounds so they can understand and think about their language and religions going back to their ancestry. Lessons on their culture may help them start to understand how privilege and White supremacy began. So begin with going back and taking some time to help your students understand that. (para. 20)

Again, Eakins is detailing work teachers can do with students; I contend, however, that teachers should apply these guidelines to themselves as a way of beginning or continuing to think about their identities.

One way to begin this work of becoming culturally competent individuals, especially if you've only begun to contend with your racial identity, is to take one of the many cultural competency self-assessments readily available online, then to use those results as a way to decide on some personal concrete action steps forward. I have appreciated the Anti-Racist Road Map (https://kateaslater.com/antiracist-roadmap) from white antiracist scholar Katie Slater, especially its call for personal accountability as a way of charting one's personal progress (Slater & Stern, 2020). It's crucial to remember that the process of becoming culturally competent is ongoing and, for many of us, life-spanning; however, it is imperative that if we are intent on creating culturally relevant intentional literacy communities and being culturally relevant educators, we must begin the work and be committed to it. We can draw inspiration from Sawdayah Brownle, farmer educator and board president of the Brooklyn Land Trust, who says, "I often remind myself that growth is not just an upward motion on a graph. It's a long, cumulative game, replete with pauses, collaborations, struggle, and blossoms. I see it as a journey and not a destination" (Weaver, 2020, para. 18).

May we be encouraged, stay committed, and keep working.

The Importance of Agreements

Fear prevents people from taking action. The worry about saying the wrong thing or, in many cases in discussions about race, being called a racist halts any words before they leave many white teachers' mouths. What we don't say, though, and what we choose to remain silent about, also speaks volumes.

I increasingly lean on the Four Agreements from Courageous Conversations About Race (Singleton, 2021) to help educators think about how to prepare themselves for critical conversations. To summarize, they are as follows:

1. Stay engaged.
2. Expect to experience discomfort.
3. Speak your truth.
4. Expect and accept a lack of closure.

I recommend attending any of the excellent workshops offered by Courageous Conversations, as they are an opportunity for professional development that deepens one's ability to engage in equity work. However, even if someone is unable to participate in a workshop, simply digging into the abundant resources available online that describe the agreements and how to use them is a powerful point of reflection and action. For instance, if we simply decide to use the agreements as a way of starting to talk about, and continuing to talk about, our developing racial understanding, we have a guardrail for how we might begin to confront our fears of "getting it wrong."

Know, too, that you *will* get "it" wrong. Frequently. Getting it wrong might mean fumbling when someone says something racist or contentious and we are immobilized. In our heads, we know we should respond, but we could spend what seems like hours silently trying to figure out exactly what that response should be or waiting for someone else to do something. So, we often say nothing. However, if we lean into the expectation of experiencing discomfort, we can act—and react—differently.

We must aim for useful responses. Silence is not useful. Silence is harmful. Dr. Beverly Daniel Tatum recommends action that includes asking questions. "The response that I tell teachers is to ask for more information," she says (i.e., "Help me to understand what you mean"). Asking for more information also disarms our own potentially defensive posture, especially if we fear being called racist or contending with students' fear of being called racist. With that curiosity, too, comes the potential for learning more. Tatum explains, "I found that when working with teachers, when they did ask that question [for more information], and they asked it sincerely, they often learn things that they weren't even aware of" (in Reich, 2020, para. 64). Shifting into an inquiry stance moves us to act: to be curious, to ask questions, and to not be a bystander. Inquiry allows us to stay engaged, and it enables us to move ahead with necessary critical conversations.

Practice Moving to Action: A Framework

Many people hesitate to have critical conversations because they lack practice. Think about it: if we are learning something, we don't expect that we're going to master it immediately—or, at least, we shouldn't expect that. Instead, proficiency takes consistent, committed practice. In my work with educators, I've been thinking about how to help them prepare for critical conversations and then practice them, something that teachers have repeatedly asked for help doing. The following reflection steps are designed to increase our facility and ability to have critical conversations, with the goal of action. I suggest first answering them honestly, then practicing them and referencing these steps as you grow more comfortable engaging in conversations about equity and other topics.

1. Check in
2. Prepare
3. Act
4. Reflect
5. Debrief

1. **Check in with yourself first.** Use tools like the Courageous Conversations Compass to identify where you are located on a particular issue. Identify your fears—write them down. Name the identities you bring to the conversation, especially the dominant ones (see Learning for Justice or Racial Equity Tools for more). Consider how your dominant identities and location on the Compass might impact how you enter the conversation.

2. **Prepare for the critical conversation.** What is the purpose of this conversation? How do you want to show up? What energy might the other person be bringing into the conversation (e.g., past experiences, especially with schooling, for instance) that you need to remember and empathize with? Where do you need to be empathetic? What and how should you listen: to understand or to respond? What power dynamics (race, gender, ability, class, etc.) do you need to acknowledge and prepare for in this conversation? What will you do if you feel yourself getting defensive? What are you afraid of in this conversation? What could you do to challenge those fears? What is the worst outcome that could result in this conversation? What tools and strategies do you have, or need to have, to be able to know you can handle having this conversation?

3. **Act.** Have the critical conversation. What is your desired outcome of the conversation? What questions do you need to ask that will indicate you hear the other person? Write them down. How will you remind yourself to breathe and recenter yourself if necessary? How might you reach an equitable agreement for you and the other person?

4. **Reflect.** Check in with yourself again once the conversation ends. How did the conversation go? Did it meet your intended

goals? If so, what specific actions did you take to make reaching the goals possible? If not, what factors got in the way? What are your next steps to keep moving toward equity? What are the other person(s)'s next steps? What are your growing edges you want to keep working on improving?

5. **Debrief.** Find someone you can trust to share your experience having this critical conversation. This person might be someone who can be an accountability partner or another trusted person who is able to hold your experiences and to help you process them.

Ultimately, there's no single way to have conversations about equity that can include race, racism, and other topics. However, if we practice, prepare, and seek out moments to speak up, we can increase our proficiency. We can also invite colleagues into our conversations and build capacity across our networks, classrooms, and communities. Becoming familiar with how to engage in these conversations and then *having them* builds our ability to normalize these types of discussions.

Now, Our Curriculum

We started with thinking through how to have critical conversations to prepare for the ongoing interactions you'll have as you decide to change your curriculum. Next, I focus on a few specific areas that help teachers move their curriculum forward: from planning prior to the year, to a midpoint check-in, to an end-of-the-year reflection. These specific strategies are intended to help teachers think through and implement consistent changes that directly impact their students.

Doing Something Differently: Before the Year Begins

If we know our students aren't reading a particular text and can vividly recall the dread you and they feel at mere mention of [insert said text here], that is enough to know that you have to do something different. We don't have to have a fully formed reason why we want to change our curriculum if we know it's not culturally relevant and if it's not addressing the students in front of us. Sometimes, a gut feeling is enough of a catalyst for change if we stop and pay attention to it. A few steps for the summer include reflecting on what we currently do, diversifying our own reading lives, and deciding to make changes to our curriculum and taking action.

At some point in my teaching career, I met my colleague, Michelle Li, who had an engineering and technology background in higher education before becoming a high school ELA teacher. She convinced me to think about teaching using the principles of design thinking, encouragement that changed my practice in powerful ways. Stanford's Design School (2021) defines *design thinking* as "a methodology for creative problem solving" (para. 01). Essentially, adopting a design thinking mindset opens up space for possibilities. Teachers are always trying something: new ideas, new texts, new ways of building community. This cycle—which includes planning, creating a prototype, trying something new, and reflecting—is useful for thinking about the teacher's work within CRILCs. If we are always thinking of our practice as dynamic, as a fertile and necessary space for regular changes to our practice, then we can also understand that we will make mistakes, develop new understandings about ourselves and our students, and always work toward improving our practice along the way. It is harder to get tied to ideas or stuck if we adapt a mindset that always insists we keep tinkering, reflecting, and revising. Adopting a design thinking mindset ultimately impacts the planning and delivery of instruction we do with students, enabling us to be more thoughtful, equitable, and effective.

We also need to be guided by the power of "radical imagination" and of doing something completely different that can change our students' lives and experiences. I'm heartened by Chicago educator Ashley McCall (2020), who asked, "What if?". . . What if we did something different, on purpose? What if we refused to return to normal?" (para. 12). We can ask ourselves those same questions when we change our curriculum, and we can lean on a future where we reimagine what literacy can look like for our students. "Normal" curriculum typically doesn't serve Black, Latinx, and other POC students well at all because the norm was designed with dominant groups in mind. If we want to value our BIPOC students as the intellectual beings they are, then we need to change our practices. Ladson-Billings (2021) believes that schooling post-COVID-19 should demand a "radical rethinking of schooling" where we query, "How else can school be?" Dismantling and rethinking our curriculum is a fitting entry point for the tangible work ELA educators can do.

Spend time in the summer before the school year begins in reflection. Be guided by scholar Maxine Greene's (2018) reminder: "A teacher in search of his/her own freedom may be the only kind of teacher who can arouse young persons to go in search of their own." Incorporating tools like Learning for Justice's (2017) *Reading Diversity: A Tool for Selecting Diverse Texts* and Tricia Ebarvia's (2019) "How Inclusive Is Your Literacy Classroom Really?" are excellent starting points for thinking through the texts we teach, might teach, and want to teach. Then, think about what the results suggest about your practices: where are opportunities for teaching for equity and for making your teaching more culturally relevant? Where can you diversify your life and your practices beyond your classroom? The tools will certainly indicate curricular gaps that need attention. Consider what you're hoping to teach in the following school year and how to address those gaps. Ground yourself in the design thinking process and commit to changing your curriculum.

The summer is also a time to read as many books as you can that may be unfamiliar to you but that are critical for making sense of our current moment and the history that got us here. This broadened reading focus is also a way to develop your own sociopolitical consciousness. You should aim to make your life as diverse as your bookshelves, reading books that are windows and developing your personal understandings. For example, annually, I read Electric Literature's "43 Books by Women of Color to Read in 2021." I add all titles to my TBR (to be read) list, with the goals of reading books that might have otherwise not been on my radar and expanding my understanding and familiarity of books that I can use with young people and with educators. I read intentionally, and I read constantly.

Summer is also a time to consider which texts need to be removed from your curriculum based on your new understandings. Actually remove them, or make an action plan to decentralize them (i.e., changing a core text to a choice text). It just might be time to retire *Adventures of Huckleberry Finn*, for instance, given its abundant use of the N-word, the difficulty of using that particular text to teach satire, and the skills needed to teach the text in a nonharmful way. This is a text that causes curriculum violence. If you have to turn yourself into knots to justify teaching or keeping the text in your scope and sequence, those feelings are powerful indicators that it's time to change your curriculum.

Fortunately, there are excellent resources that can help you make different choices about your texts. As co-founder of #disrupttexts (www.disrupttexts.org), I am guided by our core principles as I consider texts and my own identity work as an educator. While I recommend readers spend time thinking through all of our work, I draw your attention to principle 2: "Center Black, Indigenous, and voices of color" (#DisruptTexts, 2021). As we explain: "Literature study in U.S. classrooms has largely focused on the experiences of White (and male) dominated society, as perpetuated through a traditional, Euro-centric canon. Ask: What voices—authors or characters—are marginalized or missing in our study? How are these perspectives authentic to the lived experiences of communities of color?" (para. 05). Whose voices are centered and whose voices are missing in your own curriculum? Introduce those texts to your students, through core texts, classroom library additions, and choice reading.

What immediate decisions can you make during the summer to begin implementing changes in the fall? Think about what you want your students to remember long after they've left your classroom. Think, too, about the democratic citizenry they will join. What kind of readers do you want them to be? What kind of *people* do you want them to be? What texts can help everyone in your classroom fully realize those hopes and dreams? Be guided by the answers to those questions, and move to action. Release any allegiance to teaching "classics," acknowledging that far too many of our students rely on aids like SparkNotes rather than reading the assigned texts. Surely we want to guide young people to be proficient in more than the reading of those materials?

Taken in its entirety, what is the story your curriculum communicates about what you value? How would your students answer that question? Are you comfortable with the answers to this question?

It's important simply to start and to hold yourself accountable for making progress. Actionable goals that you can reevaluate throughout the year are helpful for supporting your work. Again, write those goals down in a place where they are visible and you can revisit regularly. Set reminders for when those check-ins will occur.

You might begin by replacing one core text with a diverse text during each quarter as one small step. However, deciding which texts to adopt must be a thoughtful decision. If you are seeking to provide an #ownvoice perspective about a particular subject, take the time to read widely enough that you can make an informed choice. What are the messages the potential text communicates through themes?

Are those themes in step with being culturally relevant? Also, if you decide to use a particular text, what are the lasting impacts on students? For instance, if the text is about enslavement, is this the only opportunity for readers to interact with Black voices? And, if so, then what might they associate with the "Black experience." Instead, aim for a *range* of experiences—as no group is a monolith—that makes them less susceptible to generalizing or stereotyping those experiences. You might also, simultaneously, begin diversifying your classroom library (and if you don't have a classroom library yet, you can begin building a diverse one throughout the school year).

If you begin the process of diversifying and updating your curriculum with a commitment to supporting the literacy lives of all your students, especially ones who have been historically marginalized in our classrooms, you will be able to adopt a stance of learning as you go. Only you will know how your students respond to a text. Only you will know which assessments make sense to determine if they've learned the objectives you've established as necessary to master. If you have taken the steps to create an intentional literacy community with your students, this process will be collaborative and meaningful.

You might teach a new text that doesn't land as you hoped with your students. That's OK. Because you are working in community with your students, you can discuss the experience with them and let them help you make changes and suggestions. The goal, always, is to reflect regularly on what is happening for students, and for yourself, as you make important changes to your curriculum, and to continue learning and growing.

Midpoint: Check In on Your Goals

At the conclusion of your summer planning, set a date that's the halfway point in your year to conduct a midpoint check-in on your progress. I tended to use the end of the semester, as that seemed a natural pause. What are you proud of? Building and sustaining

CRILCs is hard work; pausing to celebrate the wins, however small, is important, and it can become a routine that you can share with your students. If you've set goals for yourself about what you hoped to accomplish for the fall, particularly in response to incorporating diverse texts and having critical conversations, reflect on how that work is going. While we most likely administer all sorts of informal assessments for our students, the ones we conduct with ourselves, especially around our culturally relevant practice, are also important.

Listen to how your students have been experiencing the course. Since you've spent time building a collaborative, responsive community, they should feel comfortable giving their honest assessments throughout the term/season about the texts, the ways they feel about enacting the values and practices of the CRILCs, and what they think needs to change. My students and I had regular class meetings that were dedicated times for this feedback to occur (a routine), and I also had boxes in which students could drop anonymous feedback as they entered or exited the class (another routine).

Share your progress with your students, while also sharing what you're noticing about their feedback. Respond to what they are saying to you, even if it's hard to hear. Note: It's also important for you to also think about *why*, exactly, that feedback is hard to hear. What biases might be getting in your way that prevent your ability to digest the content and message of what your students are saying? CRILCs are accountable to everyone within them; thus, this midpoint feedback check-in is one important touchstone that assesses how the community is doing and also enables course corrections for the rest of the school year, to be read and responded to as part of an ongoing, public feedback loop.

Once you have gathered feedback from your students, your parents, and other key stakeholders (i.e., others who might interact with students throughout their day, in spaces inside and outside school), think about what changes you want to institute for the rest of the year. Consult the standards again, your summer goals, and any other timelines and structures that need to be considered (which includes state mandated testing, most likely), and set actionable goals for the remainder of your school year.

End-of-Year Audit

The conclusion of the school year invites a comprehensive reflection, a fitting pause to pull together the ongoing reflection from throughout the year. What was accomplished, particularly around making curricular changes, around developing individual and students' cultural competence, around assessing student mastery? It's time to think, again, about accountability: for the goals around racial equity and racial literacy, what was successful and what work remains, knowing there is always more work to do? How can you use the last year to inform your next steps, for yourself, your practice, and your students?

As the year comes to a close, it's time to think about how the routines and traditions of your CRILC also need attention. Perhaps students created their own traditions (highly likely) that you want to formalize, or at least introduce as possibilities, with next year's students. Or, given the design thinking mindset, perhaps parts of the curriculum or texts you've used fell flat and didn't deliver the intended impact. It's fine to consider a year as a prototype and to return to the inquiry cycle, ask different questions, and attempt different solutions. There have been years where I've replaced nearly all of my core texts in service to meeting the needs of my students, or I've changed objectives because I've noticed areas of learning where students need reinforcement, additional instruction, or acceleration.

What remains, too, is our responsibility to remain committed to the cycle of reflection, rethinking, disrupting, and creating anew, with our students. Certainly we will stumble, but it's the commitment to the practice of improvement and to holding the highest hopes for our students' academic achievement that must sustain us and continually move us forward. I'm certain that we will find that the more we internalize these cycles of interrogating our texts, replacing them, and engaging in challenging conversations about the topics they broach, the better we can become at addressing them with our students.

Takeaway

In this chapter, I've directed us toward action: action that can include preparations for critical conversations; action in deciding to make our curricula culturally relevant and responsive to students within our CRILCs; action in how we choose to think about the entire process of doing our work differently. Like much of the direction for this book, the work is focused on the teacher, who has the responsibility of creating the conditions required for CRILCs to thrive. Our students are always with us, however, and it is for them that we do the work of preparing ourselves in the many ways required to show up and be the equitable, culturally relevant teachers they need.

To-Do's

- What's the work you need to do yourself to become culturally competent? Draw on some of the tools mentioned in this chapter to deepen your understanding of yourself. How does this work strengthen your personal identity and prepare you to work with your students?
- Practice having conversations using the Framework for Productive and Equitable Critical Conversations to

increase your reaction time and comfort with having these types of discussions.

- Evaluate your curriculum using some of the resources suggested in this chapter. Then, sketch out a reenvisioned school year, inserting check-in and reflection points. How will you assure accountability for making your plan a reality?

In the final chapter, we put all of the parts together. Although we've not spent as much time talking about the students, we have spent time cultivating a robust classroom community that will enable them to thrive. Now, we turn to some specific instructional practices that strengthen and sustain our literacy work with students and that can normalize their high achievement.

6

Putting It All Together: Toward Your Transformative CRILC Practice

A personal refrain of mine lately has been that we are living in a clarifying time . . . consider who you want to be when the morning light finds you.
—Saeed Jones, "The Question Your Soul Answers"

Throughout the previous chapters, the focus was on building the capacity of teachers to understand and create the ideal conditions for making their classrooms culturally relevant intentional literacy communities. In this final chapter, I address some next steps through the following goals:

- How to address harm to students and/or community members when we are responsible;
- Discussing two high-leverage practices—discussion protocols and focused feedback—that can normalize literacy achievement for students.

The throughline for these objectives is the need to take regular, consistent action to provide the conditions that make it possible for our students to view themselves as productive, valuable members of our classrooms.

When Harm Happens

Despite our best intentions, we can create classrooms where students are harmed. Through the texts we teach, decisions we make, silences we allow—we must be prepared to respond when someone within our culturally relevant intentional literacy community experiences harm. If we are guided by the restorative justice question "What can make this as right as possible?" we can think first about our students and communities and make decisions based on *their* best interests, even if those decisions might mean ceasing to teach a beloved book, or eliminating particular assignments, or speaking up and advocating for changes at a systems-wide level.

I think we can underestimate the significance of the harm we can cause for our students. I have excerpted parts of an open letter from a young biracial Black woman who was harmed by her ELA curriculum. As you read Saoirse Herlihy's letter, think about the question of what can make what happened to her as right as possible as a way of considering what we owe our students and what we must get right in our work with them.

To Gorham (MA) educators,

Since I moved to Gorham in 1st grade, I have been simultaneously invisible and hyper-visible. My school career was defined by the fact that I was the "Black girl" and also the fact that no one wanted to acknowledge that I am a Black girl.

The boiling point of my experience was my American Literature class sophomore year. Although I found all of the texts in this class to be deeply flawed and not reflective of America, *Adventures of Huckleberry Finn* and *To Kill a Mockingbird* had the most detrimental effect on my mental health.

The fact that this serves as the text about America's brutal history of slavery in our country is wrong on more levels than I could ever articulate. First of all, it's written by a white man who has never and will never experience the systematic oppression of Black people. The only Black character in this book is a one-dimensional stereotype with no power, original thoughts, or identity.

So my question to all of you is what does this say to our Black students? I can tell you how it made me feel. It made me feel like I am one-dimensional in your eyes. It made me feel like my story is only valid if a white voice is telling it. It made me feel like I will always defer to white people no matter my age, intellect, or ability. How on earth can this text not be completely damaging and destructive to a Black person's concept of self-worth? (This is not even including the text's degrading and despicable use of the N-word.)

The text itself did enough damage, but the place where my pain took on a new level was in our class discussions. As we discussed this text, I felt an obligation to speak in order for a Black perspective to be heard. None of my classmates had had previous discussions about race beyond talking about how awesome Martin Luther King Jr. was and how he had a dream white and Black people could be friends. Meanwhile, I had spent my entire life fielding their microaggressions and being aware of racism in America. These conversations about what it meant to be Black in the United States weren't new to me. I'd been having them and living that experience my whole life.

Although the silence of my classmates rang through my ears, my teacher's silence spoke volumes too. My teacher's silence told me that even if they disagreed with what the student said, they prioritized his voice and comfort over my safety in the classroom. When racist comments like these are made, the teacher is responsible to be firmly and unapologetically anti-racist. When racism isn't acknowledged and corrected, it manifests, and who pays the price? Black people.

No one wins when texts like these are taught, and Black students like myself are left with traumatic experiences. I am just beginning to cope with the damage these titles had on my identity as a Black woman and the fact that I didn't feel safe or heard in my school system. We need books by Black authors and authors of color. We need to value intersectionality in the curriculum. We need stories that challenge the idea that whiteness is the default. I wish I had the opportunity to read about Black love, joy, and resiliency in my assigned texts, not just Black oppression and systematic racism from a white perspective. I think students across the board would benefit from reading about the multifaceted nature of the Black experience and seeing multi-dimensional characters of color.

This isn't a quick fix. The commitment to inclusion takes constant learning and work, but it's necessary to ensure that Black students feel empowered in their education and safe in their schools. (Herlihy, 2020)

Before we think about anything else, let's first consider some of the issues this young person has chronicled about her educational experience:

- Classrooms where there are only a few Black and other POC students and microaggressions occur.
- Failure to understand Black and other POC students as complex, multidimensional people.
- The lack of inclusive and expansive representation in texts selected for ELA classes; problematic, stereotyped representation in existing texts; a lack of a range of experiences that included love and joy.
- The use of the N-word.

- Expecting Black and other POC students to be the representatives for all BIPOC folks.
- White students and teachers unprepared to talk about race and racism and teachers' white silence.

I want to sit with a few of these issues as we think through harm and how to make what was done right, specifically the use of the N-word, expecting Black students to be representatives for their entire racial group, and the lack of inclusive texts or the use of texts with harmful stereotypes. And while discussing these issues and how to address them won't directly impact Saorise, it is my hope that through understanding her powerful account we can be able to prevent other students from having to experience similar educational harm.

The Use of the N-Word

It's never a positive experience to hear the N-word in a classroom setting, even if it is within the context of reading it in a text. Historian Elizabeth Stordeur Pryor (2019) says, "The six-letter word is like a capsule of accumulated hurt. Every time it is said, every time, it releases into the atmosphere the hateful notion that black people are less. (12:28). How to handle the teaching of the word, though, varies, and it is in that variance that harm happens. For instance, teachers might instruct students that they don't have to say the word if reading aloud, but the teacher might read it aloud instead (true story). Or, a teacher might permit students to write the word on posters as they "get into character" to re-create a moment from a text (another true story).

More stories abound about the misuse of the N-word in classrooms, certainly. Pryor calls these incidents "points of encounter," as "the moment you come face-to-face with the N-word." She adds that whenever and wherever those moments happen, however, "there's not a lot of space to talk about them." Pryor summarizes, "The single

most fraught site for these points of encounter is the classroom"
(10:23). It's no wonder, then, that teachers are conflicted. However,
either not talking about these points of encounter or talking about
them incorrectly inflicts substantial, lasting harm.

To make this situation right, a teacher has a few possibilities.
First, it is critical to know our own history with and of the N-word
before we also teach that history to students. If we don't personally
know the history of the word, we must learn it. If we've used the word
ourselves, that requires another level of personal reckoning. Pryor
(2019) explains, "Fundamentally, the N-word is an idea disguised as a
word: that black people are intellectually, biologically and immutably
inferior to white people ... and I think this is the most important part—
that that inferiority means that the injustice we suffer and inequality
we endure is essentially our own fault" (4:51). I appreciate Pryor's
TED Talk that details how she grappled with approaching the N-word
with her students, incorporating many of the same pedagogical moves
many of us have (e.g., writing the word but not saying it aloud, debating
the usage of the word, for instance). However, she acknowledges that
those strategies were ineffective:

> I hear from students that when the word is said during a lesson
> without discussion and context, it poisons the entire classroom
> environment. The trust between student and teacher is broken.
> Even so, many teachers, often with the very best of intentions, still
> say the N-word in class. They want to show and emphasize the
> horrors of U.S. racism, so they rely on it for shock value. Invoking it
> brings into stark relief the ugliness of our nation's past. But they
> forget the ideas are alive and well in our cultural fabric. (11:03)

Finally, Pryor explains her approach to teaching the N-word, which
offers powerful guidance for teachers: she does not say the word. Period.
She knows the history of the word, and she invites students into a discussion and their points of encounter by asking, "Why is talking about

the N-word hard?" These conversations are inevitable, and we can be prepared to have them.

Takeaway

We can take Pryor's suggestions as a starting place: To understand the history of the word. To unpack our own usage of the word and our impact of saying the word or having students say the word (not our intent—our impact, especially on our students). Recall Herlihy's open letter that help to reinforce that impact. To facilitate discussions with students about the history and usage of the word. And, finally, to simply agree to never, ever, say the word in class, regardless of who is in the room. Period.

To-Do's

Teach yourself the history of the N-word if you don't already know it. Ask yourself Pryor's questions: Why is talking about the N-word hard for you? What are your own personal points of encounter and history with the word? Also, consider what BIPOC students feel when they read or see the N-word. How does thinking about their perspectives deepen your understanding of teaching, and not teaching, the N-word?

Black and POC Students as "Race Representatives"

We know that most students attend segregated schools around the United States. That means that there's a likelihood that we could have one or two BIPOC students in a class of white students, if any at all. As someone who has often been in those situations, I'll tell you that it's quite painful to have white teachers stop a discussion to ask me what it's like being Black and . . . [insert some modifier here: poor? Female? From the South?]; then to have my white classmates turn and stare at me, waiting. It's not an exaggeration to say I have really wished the Earth would open and swallow me during those moments. Even I, who was quite adept at speaking on the spot, felt silenced and embarrassed during those times of being signaled out as a representative of all Black people.

Most days, I'm trying to be an expert in my own individual experience. I know a good amount of Black history, but I learn and amend my knowledge about that daily, and I have so much to learn and to make sure my child also learns. Throughout my K–12 experience, I was becoming who I am today; that identity was in flux. Asking me, and any other BIPOC student, to represent their race is damaging. Offering an explanation about the experience, Ronald Chennault, an associate professor in the Department of Education Policy Studies at DePaul University, says, "You're expected to represent and explain your group, be responsible for your group's actions," in an article about this issue in Learning for Justice (cited in Scruggs, 2010, para. 18). These expectations are unfair.

There are ways educators can make these situations the most right for our BIPOC students. It's important to see those students—to really know them as people, to not mix them up with the other BIPOC student in class (which happens frequently, students tell me) and to affirm them regularly. The very best educators also love their students. Educator Dr. Kiara Lee-Heart (2019), who was a Black student in honors classes, poignantly reminds us about the need to be recognized: "I know: It may be easy to forget about me because I'm the only Black one, but please don't. I am here, and so are my thoughts, my intellect and my emotions. Being ignored will crush my capacity to learn and to feel good about myself, just like it would for any other student" (para. 09). She also cautions educators not to fetishize or exoticize BIPOC students—they are humans, not projects— and to understand how white students are likely committing micro-aggressions (or macroaggressions) when teachers are not looking that must be addressed.

Takeaway

Set the stage so all students feel noticed, seen, and valued, especially BIPOC students. Center their needs and comfort so they will know you have their interests at heart. Get to know your students as individuals, and maintain a classroom community where everyone is seen, respected, and heard. Also, actively address situations—and individuals—that need additional teaching and reinforcement about expectations of what are acceptable ways of being when it comes to classroom behaviors. Be sure you are reflecting on your own approaches to behavior: Who is being punished? Who is being praised? If there are inequities, what is your role in them and what can you do to fix them?

To-Do's

- Help students get to know each other as part of the community. Get to know all students, especially your BIPOC, queer, and other marginalized students, beyond superficial efforts. How have they been experiencing their schooling? What is it *really* like for them to be a student in your class. (However, this is something to ask once you've developed a relationship with them. It's not an interrogation.) Seek to affirm them through images on your wall, art on your slide decks, and, of course, in your texts. Strive for a range of representation, too, so that BIPOC and white students can understand that there are a range of experiences, and that no group is a monolith.

- With students, name and discuss the three different types of microaggressions (Sue et al., 2007)—microassault, microinsult, and microinvalidation—and how they function. Then, explicitly name and reinforce what is not permitted in the classroom, and follow up on making sure students are practicing collaborative, liberatory community behaviors.

- Don't ignore any of your BIPOC students, especially if they are the only one in your class. Learn how to pronounce their names. Don't confuse one BIPOC student with another, and if you do make that mistake, apologize meaningfully and don't make that mistake again.

- Think, too, about pulling together groups that enable BIPOC students to share their cultural identities within spaces outside the classroom. I've had great success sponsoring the Black Women's Literary Society, a group that was open to all students interested in reading the work of Black women; talking about Blackness, femininity, and identity; and gathering to talk also about issues related to being a student. This created a space for Black (and other) students to spend time together, to celebrate, to commiserate, to discuss issues and gain support for their social and academic achievement, and to engage them in the work of a supportive intellectual community.

It's important also to think about how systemic racism functions. If there are classes (i.e., honors and AP classes) with only a few BIPOC students, it's imperative for teachers to raise questions about tracking and access and their role within that system. Also, if it's possible to group students together so they can be in a cohort for their classes (a decision to be made in consultation with families and students so they can be part of this discussion and process), that might be another way to mitigate the harm done by having only one or two isolated students in our classes as we challenge broader institutional systems simultaneously.

Damaging Texts

We need to give as much consideration to those texts so many mark as "life-changing" (which are often canonical and white) as being life-changing in *harmful* ways, especially for BIPOC students. Centering the harm done, and the lasting harm, to BIPOC students through our decisions are the important conversations to have.

The texts we choose to teach can cause more harm for students that claims of "literary merit" cannot rectify. Scholar Ibram Kendi offers the following suggestion for approaching any text, especially ones with racist ideas: "I'd advise readers to approach all books with an antiracist critical eye [because] . . . when we actively read with a critical eye, we protect ourselves from unknowingly consuming a book's hard to parse racist ideas" (Tamaki, 2021, para. 14). Kendi's words have a multilayered suggestion: that teachers must approach *any* book they are considering teaching with an antiracist eye, even before we put that text into a student's hands.

Problematic texts are ones that depict characters, settings, or themes as stereotypical or incorrect, or a text that makes BIPOC students in ways that make them feel—or has the potential to make them feel—targeted or traumatized. I recognize there are additional layers to defining problematic texts, but if we begin with these general guidelines, these questions will continue to lead to deeper levels of analysis as teachers shore up their own rationales for why they should not teach problematic texts. Next, we can use the following questions to help us decide to guide our decision making.

Should I Teach This Text? Starter Questions for Consideration

1. Who is telling the story? Is this an #ownvoices text? If not, what options exist to include a text that is written from an #ownvoices point of view instead?

2. Does the text promote harmful stereotypes of characters, settings, groups of people, and so forth? What are cultural insiders (i.e., scholars, community members, elders, etc.) saying about this text?

3. What are the identities represented by the focal group? Is this text the only representation of the focal group in the story that I teach throughout the entire year? If so, am I comfortable with this being the representative texts that students will refer to repeatedly?

4. Does this text have any harmful, racist language or concepts in it? If so, am I prepared to fully teach the context of the word(s) (e.g., the origins of the N-word) and to take a firm stand on why it's *not* OK for students, or myself, to ever use that word in our classroom?

5. Would reading this text spotlight a BIPOC, queer, or other non-white student by singling them out, by leading others in the class to seek them out for their perspective, or any other potential situations that might lead to negative identity development (racial, sexual, etc.) for the student in the classroom

community? Am I prepared to proactively prevent and address any harm that might occur with students, family, administrators, community members, or others, by accepting it as my personal responsibility to confront the harm I've done?

6. Am I fully prepared to teach the critical historical context, setting, and so on, of the text under consideration? If the text occurs in a racially diverse place, am I prepared to teach about issues of systemic racism, linguistic justice, Black and ethnic pride and joy, and more, that are also important? What additional learning must I do *in advance* before considering teaching this text?

7. What will I do when a student who is not BIPOC or part of the focal group represented in the text says something racist or harmful? How will I speak up for my students who are attacked or harmed *in the moment and after the moment*?

These questions are intended to *begin* the process of determining whether the texts we are teaching, or are considering teaching, are problematic. If a teacher cannot answer yes to a particular set of questions, it doesn't necessarily mean they shouldn't teach a text; rather, the teacher needs to take the appropriate steps to prepare themselves before returning to the rest of the questions. The aim is to think proactively about how we can prevent curriculum harm and trauma for students and become more skilled at our decisions. Once we've settled on those inclusively diverse texts, we need to guide students in how to talk about them, which is the focus of the next section.

Productive, Inclusive Discussions About Race

I've often had young people who were mystified by how discussions worked. If they'd spent any time in upper-level classes, they thought that a teacher asked a question and one or two (usually white) students would spend most of the airtime talking. The content didn't necessarily have to be in response to the teacher's question; rather, what my students tended to remember was that the speaker seemed to earn the teacher's praise or approval.

When I asked my students if they felt comfortable entering those conversations, they often didn't, thinking themselves unprepared or afraid of saying the wrong thing. As a result, lots of Black, Latinx, and other young people were sitting on the sidelines of those classroom discussions, hesitant to share their brilliance, to ask questions, or to engage at all.

Think about how discussions drive so much of our interactions throughout our lives. Now, think about the multiple parts required to prepare for and engage in a successful discussion in a classroom. Those parts might include the following:

- Having an understanding of the topic to be discussed.
- Knowing how to pose an initial question and subsequent questions.
- Figuring out how to enter the conversation (hand raising, signaling, etc.).
- Understanding how to support a point with evidence.
- Having ways to continue a discussion without relying on a teacher.
- Knowing what happens when you want to disagree or clarify a point.
- Making sure one understands key points and throughlines throughout the discussion and how to summarize those points for later synthesis.
- Guiding white students to an understanding about how they take up space and how to practice active co-conspiratorship for their BIPOC peers.

Certainly there are more nuanced parts of discussions based on varying factors, but I've found that the aspects listed here are consistent with most of the classroom discussions I've either facilitated or observed. (Figure 6.1 shares some additional resources.) Thus, if a student, particularly a non-white one who might be in predominantly white spaces or taught by teachers who don't understand their range of interactional patterns and repertoires, has no idea about how to teach any of those processes, then it makes sense that they would feel distanced and hesitant to engage. However, we can and must explicitly teach young people the skills they need to participate successfully.

Using mentor discussions. Culturally relevant intentional literacy communities demystify processes so all students can achieve academic success. CRILCs are also places that pay attention to *why* students are not doing something without blaming the students; in this case, if all students are not participating in high levels, first, ask them why and listen to their responses. Then, actively change the system and teach students how to participate, giving them regular opportunities to achieve proficiency. All the parts required to engage in a robust discussion can, and should, be taught to students so they can be active participants, especially given how much of ELA classroom discourse relies on discussions.

FIGURE 6.1

Suggested Resources for General Discussion Strategies

Graff, G., & Birkenstein, C. (2018). *They Say/I Say: The Moves That Matter in Academic Writing, High School Edition.*

Learning for Justice. (2019). *Let's Talk! Facilitating Critical Conversations with Students.*

Walsh, J., & Sattes, B. (2015). *Questioning for Classroom Discussion: Purposeful Speaking, Engaged Listening, Deep Thinking.*

Wiggins, A. (2017). *The Best Class You Never Taught: How Spiderweb Discussion Can Turn Students into Learning Leaders.*

Mentor texts, texts that we can study to learn something from, can be used to introduce discussion practices. Remind Black, Latinx, and other POC students and their peers that they most likely already *do* know how to engage in discussions. We can look to Ebonics and African American Vernacular English (AAVE) for examples. Select a short clip, between three and five minutes long, that features a discussion. The clip need not be so juicy that students will get caught up in what is said; instead, you want them to focus more on the *how* of the discussion. Thus, it's easier to do that if the topic is less familiar or of interest to them. If it's one where participants are actively engaged, students might observe the participants listening to each other, nodding heads, interrupting, exaggerating (also called signifying), and other interactional patterns common to Black speech. Even for non-AAVE speakers, deciding to use a clip of AAVE speakers having a discussion is a powerful decision: it centers and normalizes linguistic variety, especially if the teacher selects the clip as a mentor text.

From mentor texts to minilessons. Ask students what they notice about the discussion example. Be sure to draw their attention to aspects of the discussion you know you might need to create minilessons for explicit teaching later. Collect their comments on a piece of chart paper or something that allows the class to revisit their observations regularly and that can be displayed for all to see.

Teachers have a range of options after their observations: They might ask students to compare the clip to discussions they have in schools and why those classroom discussions can't be similar. They could encourage students to challenge those differences and work to create a classroom where a variety of interactional patterns are encouraged and supported. In a diverse classroom, all young people can offer their own examples of how they interact with different groups: their peers, their communities, and more. These discussions grow their sociopolitical consciousness, too, as students think about what systemic structures have led to the valuing of particular types of discussion and speech over others, and as they propose solutions, which might initially get implemented in the classroom.

From those discussions comes action. The noticings and initial discussions can become scaffolds for minilessons about classroom discussion participation. Facilitate a dialogue about what a robust, full-bodied, engaged discussion would look like, and prioritize the most important competencies for students to develop. Working backward, draft minilessons that range from 10 to 15 minutes, depending on the age of your students, that explicitly model what you want students to learn how to do, provide instruction about how to do that skill, and then offer time to practice.

Minilessons on discussions about race. Give students ongoing, consistent practice discussing critical topics, especially about race, taking time to connect texts, ideas, and our current context whenever possible. After reviewing class agreements that will guide these discussions, start with short paragraphs about current events that require students to discuss race explicitly. Use the same steps for minilessons, this time being intentional about foregrounding race. A teacher must take the time to be as thoughtful about selecting a text, about preparing themselves especially with questions students might have and where they might get stuck, about coaching and debriefing students, and about debriefing as they are with the other minilessons. Thinking of this progression as a process is also important. A teacher wants to assure no harm is done, that students have a productive discussion, and that they build their skills to be able to participate in critical conversations. Ultimately, we hope students will develop the capacity to engage in important discussions long after they've left our classrooms.

Provide students with sentence stems that help them gain familiarity with discussions about race. Some resources for stems include "Sentence Starters for Meaningful Conversations" (https://eleducation. org/resources/sentence-starters-for-courageous-conversations) and "Let's Talk! Discussing Race, Racism, and Other Critical Topics with Students" (Learning for Justice, 2019).

Practicing these skills—for both general discussions and ones about race—builds students' discussion muscles intentionally. For instance, a sequence could look as follows:

1. After being introduced to the minilesson, students work with a partner, focusing explicitly on the skill a teacher wants them to develop.

2. Once students feel comfortable with a partner, pairs can be expanded to either triads or groups of four, all focused on continued proficiency of the skill in a slightly larger group. During this time, the teacher is listening, offering feedback, and centering student reflection about how they are experiencing the process. The teacher is also able to discern implicit issues that might be emerging: student hesitancy that might break down around gender, silences from white students or BIPOC students, micro and macroggressions, and so forth. These observations can, and should, become the subject of future minilessons, where the teacher can generalize their observations to prevent spotlighting students while also communicating clear expectations about what is accepted and what is not.

3. Fishbowl discussions, or Socratic seminars, can be a next step. (See Cult of Pedagogy's "The Big List of Discussions Strategies" at https://www.cultofpedagogy.com/speaking-listening -techniques/ for more ideas.) During these practice sessions, students are able to build on their work in smaller groups with half a class of their peers. A teacher can strategically create those groups to make the experience one of successful

practice and confidence building, especially for students who have been hesitant throughout the process.

4. Reflection, coaching, and debriefing happen every step of the way. The teacher introduces topics they notice during their observations of students' practice, solicits questions students have about what is challenging for them, and also brings up issues the teacher knows are important to having equitable discussions.

It is important to remember to always be intentional about these discussions, take the time to establish authentic community, and gradually release responsibility as students become proficient. This process requires time and extensive practice. Figures 6.2 and 6.3 present steps for using mentor text as a discussion start and conducting minilessons, respectively.

FIGURE 6.2

Steps to Use a Mentor Text as Discussion Starter

1. Select a short three- to five-minute clip. This will be your mentor text. Be sure this clip is affirming and nonstereotypical. You want it to be an example of a discussion that students will be able to watch, make observations about, and learn from to participate in the process of having a discussion.

2. Frame the clip with a focus for students: to watch and see what they notice about how people are having a discussion. What are they doing? What are they saying? Have students take some brief notes about what they observe.

3. Play the clip several times, pausing for students to record their observations. This multiple viewing should provide opportunities for students to capture several impressions.

4. Debrief. Ask students what they observed. Spend some time talking through their answers and making personal connections.

5. Make an anchor chart with the characteristics students have generated, and post the chart for reference. Use this chart often as a way to remind students about the qualities of discussions, to troubleshoot, and to revise as they become more proficient. Update the chart regularly.

FIGURE 6.3

Steps for Minilessons

1. Decide on the focus for your 10–20-minute minilesson based on curricular goals and what your students need to understand at the moment.
2. Design a short lesson that introduces the goal. The lesson should have a beginning, middle, and end, with ample time for students to practice the skill, with your support and gradual release of responsibility, immediately after teaching the minilesson.
3. Teach the lesson. Model the skill you're teaching your students, aiming to make your thinking visible for them as much as possible (i.e., thinking aloud). Also, build in practice for students to use the skill/lesson goal with a partner.
4. Conclude the lesson with a brief check for understanding from all students to determine their level of understanding.
5. Practice the skill. Students have time to practice the skill independently and at different times. Think about how you can weave these skills throughout your curriculum so students can master them and transfer them to other learning opportunities.

Setting Students Up for Successful Discussions

Whenever I create these minilessons, I draft a short checklist that indicates what success looks like. For instance, if I'm aiming for students to be able to support their point with evidence in a discussion, my checklist might look like this:

A successful use of evidence in today's discussion will include at least one of the following:

- A quote from the reading or an example from your life that supports the point being made (criteria will depend on what skill students need to develop in a particular moment and time); and
- An attempt to tie your evidence to the discussion.

I focus on using positive language and isolating what skills I want students to master during a discussion as the focus for the criteria.

Then, students have time to assess themselves against the checklist, creating their own ownership over the process and self-awareness before moving into a larger discussion. Students need lots of opportunities to practice and develop their proficiency. I'd first have students practice in smaller groups (from pairs to triads), reflect on those experiences using a structured prompt, then take that feedback to tweak their participation and prepare for a whole-group discussion.

Addressing the Sociopolitical Context: Discussions About Race

Just as a teacher is drawing on mentor texts for examples of discussions, a more finite analysis of discussion patterns should also include questions about race, gender, and other identity markers. The goal of these conversations about patterns is to enable more democratic discussions that disrupt the power imbalances and that also encourage young people to participate and facilitate them. Through taking the time to intentionally break down discussions, to name the issues at play and how to dismantle them, and to provide regular practice, teachers can help students become active participants in class discussions and attain the critical learning that accompanies those interactions.

Often, just like adults, students find themselves with nothing to say in conversations about race. They struggle to find the words, to respond, or to get discussions back on track. Specific discussion stems can help students respond to issues that can arise during conversations, especially ones that attempt to derail discussions, that attack the speaker, and that help students move the discussion forward and validate harmed parties. Taking time to role-play these discussions with students is a powerful way to give them practice with the stems and also to debrief and reflect. I've adapted a few discussion stems from Autumn Brown and Danielle Sered's (n.d.) "Re-railing the Conversation on Race" and have provided explanations for their importance in our work with students.

Discussion stem: "I hear you, and I'm happy to talk about what you raised, but I'd like to finish talking about what I raised first. Can we do that?"

Explanation: In discussions, students can get sidetracked and interrupt the person they're talking to. These interruptions make it difficult for the person who is talking to continue making their point. Providing students with a way to get the discussion back on track helps them to practice being able to make their point.

Discussion stem: "What I hear you saying is. . . ."

Explanation: Everyone wants to be heard and acknowledged. Repeating back a person's words helps validate them while also helping the other person to refocus and move the conversation and move it forward.

Discussion stem: "The way you are talking about this is derailing the direction of our conversation from a point I am trying to address."

Explanation: Students need a way to get a conversation back on track and to feel empowered when they do. They also need a way to acknowledge attempts by their peers to not listen to their points, even where disagreement occurs.

Discussion stem: "Can we talk about the subject and not the way I am talking about the subject?"

Explanation: Teachers need to directly name how attacking someone for their tone (i.e., "tone policing") or emotion as they engage in discussion can be racist, sexist, and unproductive, especially when the attacks are directed at a BIPOC student, a queer student, a student with disabilities, or others who are vulnerable to having their arguments devalued based on their identity.

These discussion stems are intended to help students feel empowered in discussions about race by giving them responses that help them get unstuck. Minilessons about these discussions must also include addressing the sociopolitical contexts within which they exist: white supremacy, gaslighting, and misogynoir, among others. These discussion stems about race prepare students with responses that allow them to stay involved in critical discussions. Giving them ample time to practice these responses in discussions, while also role-playing them regularly, builds community, enables trouble-shooting, and normalizes conversations about race and other critical conversations.

Now, we think about how to provide effective feedback to our students when they (and we) inevitably make mistakes during these discussions. When those mistakes happen, they are not the end of the world; in fact, by delivering research-based feedback appropriately, we can make our CRILCs even stronger.

Delivering Quality Feedback on Discussions

Students deserve to know how they're doing in our discussions. Unfortunately, Black, Latinx, and other POC students don't always have an accurate understanding of their progress or what they need to do to improve, largely stemming from our own reluctance to (1) talk about race, (2) teach them how to have effective discussions, and (3) teach them how to tell them the truth about how they're doing in those discussions. We have to understand how to deliver feedback that leads to improvement.

Understanding the Right Type of Feedback

Our inability to tell students the truth about how to improve in class discussions is harmful. Dr. Adrian Mims, founder of the Calculus Project, explains, "Too often the feedback is embellished and not honest for various reasons. Teachers want students to perform at a high level (output) without providing them with the required (input)" (personal correspondence, 2021). Beverly Daniel Tatum offers, "White teachers in particular struggled with giving honest feedback to students of color, particularly adolescents because their fear was that either this kid or the kid's parent would perceive their negative feedback ... as somehow being racially motivated, like you're picking on my kid" (in Reich, 2020, para. 43). Additionally, researchers Yeager et al. (2014) indicate that adolescence "could be a time when minority adolescents start to draw conclusions about whether they can trust mainstream institutions like school" (p. 805). If we don't honestly tell our students, especially our Black, Latinx, and other POC students, how they are doing, we risk creating or sustaining dissonance that prevents them from accurately seeing themselves as achievers and also accurately understanding how they can improve. We can learn how to give a different type of feedback, however.

Yeager and colleagues (2014) offer the following guidance, defining it as "critical feedback":

> In theory, this can be accomplished in a feedback interaction through three steps. Critical feedback must be conveyed as a reflection of the teacher's high standards and not their bias. The student must be assured that he or she has the potential to reach these high standards, lessening the possibility that they are being viewed as limited. Students must also be provided with the resources, such as substantive feedback, to reach the standards demanded of them. These practices create a positive attributional space for students to interpret critical feedback, one that for them lessens the plausibility that the stereotype is driving their treatment. Stereotyped students can attribute the critical nature of the feedback to the instructor's high standards rather than racial bias, and they can rest assured that the instructor harbors no stereotype-based judgment of them. Further, provided with the instructional resources they need to improve, students will go on to refute the stereotype by reaching the higher standard. (p. 806)

In other words, feedback that acknowledges the complexity of the task, the student's ability to complete the work, shows them how to do the work and provides the appropriate resources leads to success. Within a culturally relevant intentional literacy community, delivering this type of feedback is ongoing and necessary for students to be able to improve continuously. Pause for a moment to think about recent feedback you gave to a BIPOC student. Did that feedback meet the criteria of Yeager et al.? Giving critical feedback regularly helps students and families always know where they stand, that they are able and expected to satisfactorily complete the task, and how to be successful.

Critical Feedback for Critical Discussions

In the process of modeling and role-playing discussions, teachers must give students effective feedback. This feedback must acknowledge the complexity of the task and that students can master that task (of having productive critical conversations with each other) and explain the explicit steps required to do the task correctly. In practice, it might look like the following:

During a discussion about a character's racist behavior in a novel, a student says something along the lines of "We should give this character a break. They didn't know any better." The student's peers remain silent. The conversation continues for a few moments after another student changes the subject and time is called.

The teacher cannot remain silent and must provide feedback for students. Using the criteria of "wise feedback," (Yeager et al., 2014) a teacher might first ask students to complete a brief written reflection about the discussion on their own, noting what came up for them after the discussion and if any questions remain. In that time, the teacher can prepare themselves to deliver feedback that will be effective.

The steps you can take for offering effective feedback are as follows:

1. **Acknowledge your high standards.** "It can be really challenging to discuss race. It's hard for most people in general, so I know it can also be hard for you all. I also know that we have spent time creating a community, addressing and repairing harm, and making sure we can all talk about issues that help us to be empowered, democratic citizens. I fully expect all of us to be able to have critical conversations about race, to stay engaged, and to be able to keep having these discussions."

2. **Affirm your and students' belief in them**. "I know you can have these discussions. They take time and practice, and I'm not going to give up on you as we learn how."

3. **Deliver feedback**. "In the discussion we just had, I noticed that when someone made a comment about a character's racist behavior, no one spoke up. I'm interested to know your take on that." Let students offer any feedback from their written reflections. Don't rush. Be comfortable sitting in silence. Wait. Then, continue: "When we don't speak up about something that's racist, our silence can be read as agreement with the speaker, action, or event. That's not OK. Even if you didn't know what to say in that moment, you have question stems that you can use. For example, one might be 'Can you help me to understand what you meant when you said . . . ?' Asking that question helps the speaker explain their thinking while also opening up the conversation for broader discussion and analysis, which is the goal of our classroom discussions. What other questions could you ask? If you could go back to that discussion, what could you have done differently? What else can you say when we have our next discussion about our reading and an issue comes up again? Saying nothing is not

OK." As students generate suggestions, you can write these on the board and add any other resources for students.

4. **Conclude the feedback session.** Check in with students to see if there are remaining questions and also provide a space (e.g., an anonymous feedback box) for students to provide any comments they want to give only to you. Reiterate to students the challenge of having critical conversations about race and other topics and your belief in their ability to have them, and the opportunities that come from having these discussions. Then, remind students about the responses they've generated, and end with the expectation that they have the resources to draw on and continue practicing and working toward mastery in subsequent discussions.

In a culturally relevant intentional literacy community, students receive regular feedback about their participation in critical discussions. From the beginning, the teacher has worked to create a collaborative understanding of expectations; thus, conversations about progress are ongoing and generative and do not shame students. All students are expected to make steady progress on their discussion goals because proficiency makes everyone in the community capable of engaging in these types of discussions. The teacher stands ready to guide, coach, model, and slowly hand over more responsibility to students as they become more proficient. The teacher is also able to address issues of racism and power imbalances in small and larger groups as needed.

Students receive clear feedback about what they need to do to make progress. Both the student and the teacher are clear about what progress looks like, what the student needs to do to make that progress, and what resources are available to make the progress. The teacher's feedback helps keep the student on target. Because students know the teacher believes in them and expects them to make that progress, coupled with the teacher showing them *how* to make that progress, they are more likely to truly receive and act upon that feedback.

This type of feedback is different from what has been termed "dysfunctional rescuing," whereby a teacher might swoop in when students exhibit discomfort or uncertainty about completing a task. Rescuing students also places the teacher in a position of becoming a savior to their students rather than providing feedback that helps students internalize what they need to do to succeed. By centering "wise feedback" within CRILCs, teachers can immediately begin to normalize discussions involving race and other critical topics, assuring students have the competencies to engage in and lead productive and powerful discussions.

Takeaway

After preparing ourselves, we must have actual critical conversations with our students that involve race, racism, and other issues of the day. With the right tools, including those shared in this chapter, we can lead students through discussions that are productive for everyone in the room and inclusive of students who may have previously felt unwelcome. As we provide feedback along the way that helps students understand that we believe in them and their ability to engage in these discussions, we also solidify our culturally relevant intentional literacy communities as places where challenging conversations can lead to understanding, healing, and change for all of our students.

Final Words

You wanna fly, you got to give up the shit that
weighs you down.
—Toni Morrison, Song of Solomon

In this book, I've brought together my successful experiences as an ELA teacher of primarily Black and Latinx students in city schools. In our classrooms, we had to lean hard into getting to know each other, being vulnerable, healing ourselves, and doing the hard work of helping everyone become, or continue becoming, a literacy high achiever. Establishing and maintaining a community that was equitable and liberatory required intentional, ongoing work, and remains the most important work I've done in my educational career. More than anything else, I expected the young people I worked with to love reading, and it was my responsibility to remove barriers to their literacy achievement (while admitting that sometimes *I* was the barrier). I also wanted them to feel and know we were all responsible for one another and that I genuinely believed in them and loved them.

I have been able to make my classrooms places where we can talk about issues including race, move to action to dismantle inequities, and be in collaboration with one another. In the process, I have developed my own competence as a culturally relevant educator, more keenly focused on working in collaborative communities as we all pursue liberation. I've also had to remember that this process of liberation is not linear, but, when done in community with both students and adults, it is sustainable, possible, and necessary.

I hope *Literacy Is Liberation* provides some tangible solutions for your work with your own students. Educators have been telling me that they want to have critical conversations with students and that they want to make all children, especially our BIPOC students, know they belong in their classrooms. I believe in you, and I hope this book will be a supportive resource. Our students are already having these conversations, after all, as they envision and create the worlds they deserve. May we work beside them, together. Don't let them down.

In solidarity.

Acknowledgments

I am grateful to have always been held in communities of loving care that have enabled me to write *Literacy Is Liberation*.

My grandparents, Beulah and Robert, who taught me to read, who told me I could do whatever I set my mind to, who enabled me to love learning and literacy, and who nurtured my interior life were creators of my first community. For my mother, Karen, who loved me the best she could when I was younger, and who loves me in all the ways I'm learning to need now. For my siSTARS: Brooklyn, who never fails to come through with the right advice, insight, or joke and whose wisdom about mothering has been some of the very best. May you receive all the blessings back to you for the immense goodness you put into the world. Ashley, who has carved out her own place in the world and it's one that is good and amazing and all your own. My niece and nephews: Chloe, Caleb, and Clinton. You three provide such great energy, hilarity, and love. I am so proud of you and also so glad that Elliott has you to grow up with and to know that Kentucky is always our home. I hope you will range widely and freely as you grow and move through the world and take up all the space you want. To my aunts and uncles, especially Denice, Shawn, and Joel, steadfast supporters all these years. To Erica: you're my person. I love you. Here's to horizons of endless possibilities and revolutionary futures, always with you. And forever thanks, to my sun, Elliott. All of this is for you. Thank you for picking me to be your mom and for showing me, daily, how to live and build the world you and, we, all need. I love you the most.

To the friends who have become my chosen family: Shaunya and Robert. My Boston day-ones! We have shared so many moments, been there for each other, and come back together, all to a 90s R&B soundtrack. We remain. I love that we have each other as we walk this path (and that Shaun is walking it faster than we are, lol. #allshadealltea). To Tricia Ebarvia, thank you for your generosity that made my teaching stronger and my advocacy clearer. Anna Osborn, you live the research and practice of literacy daily, in such a powerful way that honors and sees children of color. May we all fight for kids and their literacy lives as you have. Tiana Silvas, whether it's talking about writing, sharing the incredible work your students composed, or chatting about seven-year-olds: you are honest, loyal, true. Your thoughtful surprises in the mail have kept me going over these years, and I appreciate them, and you, with all my heart. Aeriale Johnson. My kindred spirit who has become such a wonderful confidante, mirror *and* window, and true friend. You speak up and say the things that need to be voiced, and you model how to be unapologetically yourself. #squad forever! Julia Torres and Lorena German, my #DisruptTexts cofounders: thank you for modeling fierce solidarity and community. Michelle Li introduced me to so many ideas and practices that have made me a better human being, most important of them the willingness to believe in myself and to always ask questions about my own assumptions. You're the perfect companion to burn it all down with any day, and I thank you for reminding me to be brave enough to start again and again, and again.

Dr. Nicholas and Lisa Lynn have held my center, from when I was growing up in Kentucky to the present. I adore you both. You have always been my home and my family. Thank you. From the moment I talked to you on an actual phone and then met you in the aisle of a Houston Walgreens, there was just something about you, Kate Mehok, that destined us to be friends. You are the person who has known me through all the iterations of who I was becoming. You have always known the importance of just showing up, and that reliability has taken us all over the country, in various cars, in the most delightful and perplexing of situations, and you stayed. I remember every single kind gesture you've made throughout these years and am filled with so much gratitude for you and our friendship. Allan Ferola, you're my financial north star who is also a life coach, and you're so good at it! Thank you for being on my board of advisors and being so honest and so consistent in your belief in me and your insistence that I learn to manage my own life, stepping aside while I've figured that out, and always being willing to coach, cheer, and laugh along with me on the journey.

I am honored to know educators who are the very best at what they do, and who, because they care about young people and our profession, took the time to mentor me as I became the teacher I always dreamed of being. Michele Leong was my colleague for two years and did an admirable job of creating a sense of belonging while I gained confidence in the classroom. I most love that she modeled the importance of intersectional accomplices and continues to be one. Catherine Nicastro kept sending me the perfect poems over the years, knowing that the right words, in the right moment, can be exactly the salve my soul needs. Dr. Joseph R. Rodriguez is a friend of my mind and heart, always encouraging, always generous, always loving our children and teaching them well. Thank you for always nudging me to keep writing, to just sit down and try, and for telling me that the world was waiting for my words.

I've had the extraordinary blessing to have the mentors and teachers that loved me and pushed me to be, and do, my very best. To Drs. Violet J. Harris and Arlette I. Willis: you always were willing to help me think through ideas, to challenge me to dig deeper, to confront myself, and to always keep the needs of real children and teachers at the core of my work. You also mothered me deeply and loved me through my time with you and continue to encourage me from afar. Thank you for your mentorship. Dr. Theresa Perry, from the moment we met all those years ago, you saw something in me that I couldn't even dare to see in myself. Over the years, your unfailing encouragement, wisdom, and faith have pushed me to explore heights I would have never imagined for myself. Thank you for holding such a steady belief in me.

To the ASCD team, Allison Scott and Megan Doyle. Allison, your quiet persistence, ability to sketch out this book in a way that convinced me I could actually do it, and your encouragement along the way helped make this such a positive project! I will also be grateful, always, for the well-placed *Pride and Prejudice* comments that made me giggle and keep writing. Megan, thank you for picking up the baton after Allison passed it to you and keeping the book moving along. You were the ideal combination of cheerleader and warm demander. I appreciate your patience and confidence in this project.

A final thank you to the biggest community I've ever been fortunate to belong: that of the young people I've worked with and learned from over the years. Thank you for trusting me with your reading lives, with your brilliant selves, and believing that, together, we could change the world. I know you're out there doing just that, and I'm so very proud of you.

Appendix

Resources: Finding Diverse Texts

How to Use This Resource

This is not meant to be an exhaustive list; rather, this is a way to begin your understanding of diverse children's and young adult literature. Hopefully you'll be inspired to continue that literacy journey well beyond these lists.

The resources that follow are ones I use regularly to find books by the authors and illustrators of a particular group. I also follow many individual authors and illustrators on their social media pages as another way of keeping current about forthcoming titles and other texts of interest. Finally, I have tried to focus on resources that are representative of the group they write about (e.g., African American resources are written and published by African American authors and illustrators).

A General Starting Place

Cooperative Children's Book Center diversity resources:
https://ccbc.education.wisc.edu/literature-resources/diversity
-resources-multicultural-literature

We Need Diverse Books resources: https://diversebooks.org/resources

African American Children's Literature

Black Children's Books and Authors: https://bcbooksandauthors.com

The Brown Bookshelf: https://thebrownbookshelf.com

Asian American Children's Literature

Asian/Pacific American Libraries Association Literature Awards:
www.apalaweb.org/awards/literature-awards

Social Justice Books: https://socialjusticebooks.org/booklists/asian
-americans

Latinx Children's Literature

¡Colorín Colorado!: https://www.colorincolorado.org/books-authors

Latinx in Kid Lit: https://latinosinkidlit.com

Native American/Indigenous Literature

Children of the Glades (Twitter): https://twitter.com/ofglades

Heartdrum, books by Native American Authors: www.harpercollins
.com/collections/heartdrum-books-by-native-american-authors

Dr. Debbie Reese, American Indians in Children's Literature:
https://americanindiansinchildrensliterature.blogspot.com

Oyate: https://oyate.org

Queer Children's Literature

American Library Association Stonewall Award Winners:
www.ala.org/rt/rrt/award/stonewall/honored

Flamingo Rampant Press: www.flamingorampant.com

Hope in a Box: www.hopeinabox.org

Resources: Building Historical Understandings

White Rage, Carol Anderson (YA version also available)

The Fire Next Time, James Baldwin

Slavery by Another Name, The Re-enslavement of Black Americans from Slavery to World War II, Douglas A. Blackmon

Racism Without Racists: Color-Blind Racism and the Persistence of Inequality in America, Eduardo Bonilla-Silva

Black Feminist Thought, Knowledge, Consciousness and the Politics of Empowerment (2nd edition), Patricia Hill Collins

On Intersectionality: Essential Writings, Kimberlé Crenshaw

Never Caught: The Washingtons' Relentless Pursuit of Their Runaway Slave, Ona Judge, Erica Armstrong Dunbar (YA version also available)

Stony the Road: Reconstruction, White Supremacy, and the Rise of Jim Crow, Henry Louis Gates (YA version also available)

Begin Again: James Baldwin's America and Its Urgent Lessons for Our Own, Eddie Glaude, Jr.

Black Radical: The Life and Times of William Monroe Trotter, Kerri Greenidge

Ain't I a Woman, Black Women and Feminism, bell hooks

Nobody: Casualties of America's War on the Vulnerable from Ferguson to Flint and Beyond, Marc Lamont Hill

From the War on Poverty to the War on Crime: The Making of Mass Incarceration in America, Elizabeth Hinton

A Time to Break Silence: The Essential Works of Martin Luther King, Jr. for Students, Martin Luther King, Jr. and Walter Dean Myers

Sister Outsider, Audre Lorde

Forgotten Readers: Recovering the Lost History of African American Reading Societies, Elizabeth McHenry

Pushout: The Criminalization of Black Girls in School, Monique Morris

Playing in the Dark, Toni Morrison

Radical Equations: Civil Rights from Mississippi to the Algebra Project, Robert Moses and Charles Cobb

The Condemnation of Blackness: Race, Crime, and the Making of Modern Urban America, Khahil Muhammad

So You Want to Talk About Race, Ijeoma Oluo

The History of White People, Neil Painter

I've Got the Light of Freedom: The Organizing Tradition and the Mississippi Freedom Struggle, Charles Payne

Breathe: A Letter to My Sons, Imani Perry

A Black Women's History of the United States, Daina Raimey and Kali Gross

They Were Her Property: White Women as Slave Owners in the American South, Stephanie Jones-Rogers

The Color of Law: A Forgotten History of How Our Government Segregated America, Richard Rothstein

Why Are All the Black Kids Sitting Together in the Cafeteria? (revised edition), Beverly Daniel Tatum

The Myth of Seneca Falls: Memory and the Women's Suffrage Movement, 1848–1898, Lisa Tetrault

The Autobiography of Malcolm X, Malcolm X with Alex Haley

References

Advancement Project. (2012). Participatory asset mapping: A community research lab toolkit. https://www.communityscience.com/knowledge4equity/AssetMappingToolkit.pdf

Alim, S., & Paris, D. (Eds.). (2017). *Culturally sustaining pedagogies: Teaching and learning for justice in a changing world.* Teachers College Press.

Aronson, B., & Laughter, J. (2016). The theory and practice of culturally relevant education: A synthesis of research across content areas. *Review of Educational Research, 86*(1), 163–206. https://doi.org/10.3102/0034654315582066

Ayers, C. (2020, September 11). Facing race: A conversation with Seattle author Ijeoma Oluo. https://www.king5.com/article/news/community/facing-race/seattle-author-ijeoma-oluo-so-you-want-to-talk-about-race-racism/281-a2902160-afc7-4784-a177-94e861634749

Bishop, R. S. (1990, Summer). Mirrors, windows, and sliding glass doors. *Perspectives: Choosing and Using Books for the Classroom, 6*(3).

Black Liberation Collective. (n.d.). Our principles. http://www.blackliberationcollective.org/our-beliefs

Brown, A. M. (2021, April 21). Getting curious with Jonathan Van Ness & Adrienne Maree Brown. [Transcript] https://c72f5c2d-1ae7 -4c2f-9561-2c4145d468e9.filesusr.com/ugd/942720 _e9ed7fc42e59426b8db903cc92fc230c.pdf

Brown, A., & Sered, D. (n.d.). *Re-railing the conversation on race.* https://www.dvc.edu/faculty-staff/racial-justice/pdfs /Rerailing%20Race%20Talk.pdf

Brown, B. (2020). The dare to lead glossary: Key language, skills, tools, and practices. Brene Brown, LLC. https://daretolead.brenebrown.com/

Brown, V. (2019). Facilitating critical conversations. Workshop. August 17, Framingham, MA.

Conference on College Composition and Communication. (2020). *This ain't another statement! This is a DEMAND for Black linguistic justice!* https://cccc.ncte.org/cccc/demand-for-black-linguistic-justice

Cult of Pedagogy. (2020, June). Why white students need multicultural and social justice education. *Cult of Pedagogy, 7.* https://www. cultofpedagogy.com/white-students-multicultural-ed/

Dankowski, T. (2020, June 24). Ridding schools of reading trauma. *American Libraries.* https://americanlibrariesmagazine.org/blogs/the-scoop /116407/

Deep Center. (2020). Building a restorative community: Recommendations. https://www.deepcenter.org/deepcenter/wp-content/uploads/2020 /11/2020-Deep-Policy-Brief-FINAL_digital-1.pdf?utm_source=The +Deep+Dish+%28the+monthly+dish+on+all+things+Deep%29&utm _campaign=4f270cb592-EMAIL_CAMPAIGN_2018_12_19_06_55 _COPY_01&utm_medium=email&utm_term=0_ac676b6462-4f270cb592 -1304190710

Dismantling Racism. (2021). White supremacy culture. https://www. dismantlingracism.org/white-supremacy-culture.html

#DisruptTexts. (2021, January 2). *January 2021 statement.* https:// disrupttexts.org/2021/01/02/january-2021-statement/

Duyvis, C. (2015, September 6). https://twitter.com/corinneduyvis/status /640584099208503296

Dweck, C. (2006). *Mindset: The new psychology of success.* Ballantine.

Eakins, S. (2020, June 7). Why white students need multicultural and social justice education. https://www.cultofpedagogy.com/white-students -multicultural-ed/

Ebarvia, T. (2019). Keynote address. (Presentation, International Literacy Association, New Orleans, LA, October 12, 2019).

Ebarvia, T. (2021). *How inclusive is your literacy classroom really?* https://blog.heinemann.com/heinemann-fellow-tricia-ebavaria-inclusive-literacy-classroom-really

Ed Glossary. (2015). Hidden curriculum. https://www.edglossary.org/hidden-curriculum/

Electric Literature. (2021, January 6). 43 books by women of color to read in 2021. https://electricliterature.com/44-books-by-women-of-color-to-read-in-2021/

Everett, C. (2018, November 11). Beyond our shelves. *ImagineLit.* http://www.imaginelit.com/news/2018/11/25/beyond-our-shelves

Farmer, G. (2020, August 6). How schools and teachers can get better at cultural competence. *Education Next.* https://www.educationnext.org/how-schools-teachers-can-get-better-cultural-competence/

Fay, L. (2019, August 7). 74 Interview: Researcher Gloria Ladson-Billings on culturally relevant teaching, the role of teachers in Trump's America and lessons from her two decades in education research. https://www.the74million.org/article/74-interview-researcher-gloria-ladson-billings-on-culturally-relevant-teaching-the-role-of-teachers-in-trumps-america-lessons-from-her-two-decades-in-education-research/

Franklin, J. H. & Higginbotham, E. (1974). *From slavery to freedom: A history of African Americans.* Alfred A. Knopf.

Gay, G. (2013). Teaching to and through cultural diversity. *Curriculum Inquiry, 43 (1),* 48–70. DOI: 10.1111/curi.12002

Gay, G., & Banks, J. A. (2010). *Culturally responsive teaching: Theory, research, and practice.* Teachers College Press.

Gay, R. (2020, May 30). Remember, no one is coming to save us. *New York Times.* https://www.nytimes.com/2020/05/30/opinion/sunday/trump-george-floyd-coronavirus.html?action=click&module=Opinion&pgtype=Homepage

Gorman, A. (2021). Poet Amanda Gorman reads "The Hill We Climb." https://www.youtube.com/watch?v=Wz4YuEvJ3y4

Greene, M. (2018). The dialectic of freedom. Teachers College Press.

Greenidge, K. (2021, January). They say this isn't America. For most of us, it is. *Harper's Bazaar.* https://www.harpersbazaar.com/culture/politics/a35153881/they-say-this-isnt-america-trump-insurrection/

Hagopian, J. (2020, August 22). Teaching for Black lives during the rebellion. *Rethinking Schools.* [Webinar].

Haley, A., & X, M. (1965). *The autobiography of Malcolm X.* Ballantine Publishing Group.

Herlihy, S. (2020, June 11). Open letter to my high school. https://www.saoirseherlihy.com/blog/2020/6/11/open-letter-to-my-high-school

Hoxby, C. & Avery, C. (2012). The missing "one-offs": The hidden supply of high-achieving, low-income students. National Bureau of Economic Research. Cambridge, MA. https://www.nber.org/system/files/working_papers/w18586/w18586.pdf?utm_campaign=PANTHEON_STRIPPED&amp%3Butm_medium=PANTHEON_STRIPPED&amp%3Butm_source=PANTHEON_STRIPPED

Jones, S. (2020, Spring). Ending curriculum violence. *Learning for Justice, 64.* https://www.learningforjustice.org/magazine/spring-2020/ending-curriculum-violence

Kaba, M. (2021). We do this 'til we free us: Abolitionist organizing and transforming justice. Haymarket Books.

Kendi, I. X. (2019). *How to be an anti-racist.* Penguin Random House.

Ladson-Billings, G. (1995). Toward a theory of culturally relevant pedagogy. *American Educational Research Journal, 32*(3),465–491. doi:10.3102/00028312032003465

Ladson-Billings, G. (2001). *Crossing over to Canaan: The journey of new teachers in diverse classrooms.* Jossey-Bass.

Ladson-Billings, G. (2014). Culturally relevant pedagogy 2.0: a.k.a. the Remix. *Harvard Educational Review, 84*(1), 74–84.

Ladson-Billings, G. (2021, January 23). "Justice matters": Reclaiming a fundamental right with Dr Gloria Ladson-Billings and Sakeena Everett. https://www.youtube.com/watch?v=m3W8_zt7V_4&t=55s

Learning for Justice. (2019, September 21). Let's talk! https://www.learningforjustice.org/magazine/publications/lets-talk

Lee-Heart, K. (2019, September 25). A crooked seat at the table: Black and alone in an honors class. Learning for Justice. https://www.learningforjustice.org/magazine/a-crooked-seat-at-the-table-black-and-alone-in-an-honors-class

Love, B. (2019). *We want to do more than just survive: Abolitionist teaching and the pursuit of educational freedom.* Beacon.

Lyons, A. (n.d.). 5 principles of restorative justice for your community, school, or organization. Crisis and Trauma Resource Institute. https://ca.ctrinstitute.com/blog/5-principles-of-restorative-justice/

McCall, A. (2020, July 30). What if we radically reimagined the new school year? Chicago Unheard. https://chicagounheard.org/blog/what-if-we -radically-reimagined-the-new-school-year/

McKesson, D. (2018). *On the other side of freedom: The case for hope.* Penguin.

Miller, E T., & Tanner, S, J. (2019) "There can be no racial improvisation in white supremacy": What we can learn when anti-racist pedagogy fails. *Journal of Curriculum and Pedagogy, 16*(1), 72–96. doi: 10.1080 /15505170.2018.1525448

Milner, H. R. (2020, April). Fifteenth Annual AERA Brown Lecture in Education Research: Disrupting punitive practices and policies: Rac(e)ing back to reaching, teacher preparation, and *Brown. Educational Researcher, 49*(3), 147–160. doi:10.3102/0013189X20907396

Moll, L., Amanti, C., Neff, D., & Gonzalez, N. (1992). Funds of knowledge for teaching: Using a qualitative approach to connect homes and classrooms, *Theory into Practice, 31*(2), 132–141. doi: 10.1080/00405849209543534

Morrell, E. [@ernestmorrell]. (2021, April 23). What if we asked every kid in America next fall as an assignment . . . [Tweet]. https://twitter.com /ernestmorrell/status/1385537623347929089.

Morris, M. (2015). *Pushout: The criminalization of Black girls in schools.* New Press.

Murray, I., & Milner, H. (2015). Toward a pedagogy of sociopolitical conscious- ness in outside of school programs. *Urban Review, 47.* doi: 10.1007 /s11256-015-0339-4

National Council of Teachers of English. (2018a, October 25). *Literacy assessment: Definitions, principles, and practices.* https://ncte.org /statement/assessmentframingst/

National Council of Teachers of English. (2018b). *The students' right to read.* https://ncte.org/statement/righttoreadguideline/

National Council of Teachers of English. (2019a). *The act of reading: Instructional guidelines and policy guidelines.* Position statement. https://ncte.org/statement/the-act-of-reading/

National Council of Teachers of English. (2019b, November 7). *Definition of literacy in a digital Age.* https://ncte.org/statement/nctes-definition -literacy-digital-age/

National Council of Teachers of English. (2019c). *Independent reading.* https://ncte.org/statement/independent-reading/

National Council of Teachers of English. (2021). *Statement on classroom libraries.* https://ncte.org/statement/classroom-libraries/

Pernell, E. (2020). Teaching about race when there are only a few BIPOC students in class. https://www.ericapernell.com/teaching-race-bipoc

Perry, T., Steele, C., & Hilliard, A., III. (2003). *Young, gifted, and black: Promoting high achievement among African American students.* Beacon.

Pryor, E. S. (2019, December). *Why it's so hard to talk about the N-word.* https://www.ted.com/talks/elizabeth_stordeur_pryor_why_it_s_so _hard_to_talk_about_the_n_word

Reading diversity. (2016, January 25). *Learning for justice.* https:// www.learningforjustice.org/magazine/publications/reading-diversity

Reich, J. (2020, May 22). Dr. Beverly Daniels Tatum reboot. *TeachLab with Justin Reich.* https://teachlabpodcast.simplecast.com/episodes /dr-tatum-reboot/transcript

Reynolds, J., & Kendi, I. (2020). *Stamped: Racism, antiracism, and you.* Little, Brown.

Scruggs, A—O. (2010, January 11). The only one. *Learning for Justice.* https:// www.learningforjustice.org/magazine/spring-2010/the-only-one

Sealey-Ruiz, Y. (2021). Racial literacy: A policy research brief. National Council of Teachers of English. https://ncte.org/wp-content/uploads /2021/04/SquireOfficePolicyBrief_RacialLiteracy_April2021.pdf

Showing Up for Racial Justice. (n.d.). White supremacy culture. www.showingupforracialjustice.org/white-supremacy-culture.html

Singleton, G. (2021). Courageous conversations about race: A field guide for achieving equity in schools and beyond (3rd ed.). Corwin.

Slater, K., & Stern, M. (2020). 2021 Anti-racist roadmap. https://static1. squarespace.com/static/5f3f08b8ce35136b743f545a/t/5ff0be24232e037 c668c85f6/1609612837089/2021-Anti-Racist-Roadmap.pdf

Stanford Design School. (2021). Get started with design thinking. https:// dschool.stanford.edu/resources/getting-started-with-design-thinking

Stevenson, B. (2014). *Just mercy: A story of justice and redemption.* Spiegel & Grau.

Sue, D. W., Capodilupo, C. M., Torino, G. C., Bucceri, J. M., Holder, A. M. B., Nadal, K. L., & Esquilin, M. (2007). Racial microaggressions in everyday life: Implications for clinical practice. *American Psychologist, 62*(4), 271–286. doi: org/10.1037/0003-066X.62.4.271

Tamaki, J. (2021, February 25). Ibram X. Kendi likes to read at bedtime. *New York Times.* https://www.nytimes.com/2021/02/25/books/review /ibram-x-kendi-by-the-book-interview.html

Tolson, N. (2021, March 31). *A historical perspective and hope-filled future of black stories and storytellers.* Highlights Foundation. Webinar.

Tovani, C. (June 10, 2016). Keynote presentation. North Texas Council of Teachers of English Language Arts Conference. Hurst, TX.

Upping the Anti. (2005). Revolution as a mew beginning: An Interview with Grace Lee Boggs. *Upping the Anti, 1*(1), 15–29.

Weaver, D. (2020, May 1). Stories of resilience. https://www.highmowingseeds.com/blog/stories-of-resilience/

Wiggins, G., & McTighe, J. (2005). *Understanding by Design: Expanded second edition.* Pearson.

Yeager, D. S., Purdie-Vaughns, V., Garcia, J., Apfel, N., et al. (2014). Breaking the cycle of mistrust: Wise interventions to provide critical feedback across the racial divide. *Journal of Experimental Psychology: General, 143*(2), 804–824. doi: 10.1037/a0033906

Index

About the Author

Kimberly N. Parker, PhD, is an award-winning educator who has been working in literacy communities with young people for more than 20 years. She has always held a steadfast belief in the power of literacy to normalize the high achievement of all students, especially Black, Latinx, and other students of color. In a career that has included public school teaching, preparing preservice teachers, conducting research about how to develop environments that support the success of Black boy readers, and delivering professional development across the country, Kim has remained rooted in her commitment to building intentional literacy communities with and for Black and Latinx young people and supporting the work of educators. She is currently the director of the Crimson Summer

Academy at Harvard University, the 2020 recipient of the National
Council of Teachers of English (NCTE) Outstanding Elementary Educator Award, a cofounder of the grassroots movements #DisruptTexts
and #31DaysIBPOC, and the current president of the Black Educators'
Alliance of MA (BEAM). Follow her on Twitter @TchKimpossible.

Related ASCD Resources: Equity

At the time of publication, the following resources were available (ASCD stock numbers in parentheses).

Print Products

Becoming the Educator They Need: Strategies, Mindsets, and Beliefs for Supporting Male Black and Latino Students by Robert Jackson (#119010)

Cultural Competence Now: 56 Exercises to Help Educators Understand and Challenge Bias, Racism, and Privilege by Vernita Mayfield (#118043)

The Equity and Social Justice Education 50: Critical Questions for Improving Opportunities and Outcomes for Black Students by Baruti K. Kafele (#121060)

The Innocent Classroom: Dismantling Racial Bias to Support Students of Color by Alexs Pate (#120025)

Making Curriculum Matter: How to Build SEL, Equity, and Other Priorities into Daily Instruction by Angela Di Michele Lalor (#122007)

Teaching to Empower: Taking Action to Foster Student Agency, Self-Confidence, and Collaboration by Debbie Zacarian and Michael Silverstone (#120006)

Teaching with Empathy: How to Transform Your Practice by Understanding Your Learners by Lisa Westman (#121027)

Why Are We Still Doing That? Positive Alternatives to Problematic Teaching Practices by Pérsida Himmele and William Himmele (#122010)

For up-to-date information about ASCD resources, go to **www.ascd.org**. You can search the complete archives of *Educational Leadership* at **www.ascd.org/el**.

ASCD myTeachSource®

Download resources from a professional learning platform with hundreds of research-based best practices and tools for your classroom at http://myteachsource.ascd.org

For more information, send an email to member@ascd.org; call 1-800-933-2723 or 703-578-9600; send a fax to 703-575-5400; or write to Information Services, ASCD, 1703 N. Beauregard St., Alexandria, VA 22311-1714 USA.

THE WHOLE CHILD

The ASCD Whole Child approach is an effort to transition from a focus on narrowly defined academic achievement to one that promotes the long-term development and success of all children. Through this approach, ASCD supports educators, families, community members, and policymakers as they move from a vision about educating the whole child to sustainable, collaborative actions.

Literacy Is Liberation relates to the **safe**, **engaged**, and **supported** tenets. *For more about the ASCD Whole Child approach, visit* **www.ascd.org/wholechild**.

WHOLE CHILD
TENETS

1 **HEALTHY**
Each student enters school healthy and learns about and practices a healthy lifestyle.

2 **SAFE**
Each student learns in an environment that is physically and emotionally safe for students and adults.

3 **ENGAGED**
Each student is actively engaged in learning and is connected to the school and broader community.

4 **SUPPORTED**
Each student has access to personalized learning and is supported by qualified, caring adults.

5 **CHALLENGED**
Each student is challenged academically and prepared for success in college or further study and for employment and participation in a global environment.